BUILDERS OF OUR COUNTRY

BOOK I

BUILDERS OF OUR COUNTRY

BOOK I

by

Gertrude Van Duyn Southworth

YESTERDAY'S CLASSICS

ITHACA, NEW YORK

ISBN: 978-1-59915-232-5

Yesterday's Classics, LLC
PO Box 339
Ithaca, NY 14851

CONTENTS

CONTENTS

I

LEIF THE LUCKY

The Northmen and Leif the Lucky

WAY, way in the far north, in the land of ice and snow, dwelt the Norsemen or Northmen. A bold, daring race, they knew no fear. They plowed the mighty waves of the sea in their small open vessels and made war on the strongest nations, with no thought of the dangers that they faced.

The Northmen had blue eyes and golden hair. They were so tall and powerfully built that when they went into battle they seemed almost like an army of giants. Imagine how they must have looked in their coats of mail, sharp swords hanging from their belts, and on their heads helmets of iron or steel. The sides of these helmets were adorned with wings, and between the wings was an image of some fierce-looking animal. Is it to be wondered that these Northmen were the most dreaded of fighters?

On the sea they were the bravest of sailors. Their ships were small and open, only about fifty feet long, but strongly built and seaworthy. They were low in the center, curving up toward the stern and the bow; and on the bow was carved either a dragon or a sea monster.

They carried terror—these little vessels—to the people who watched their ugly bows plunging slowly through the waves and coming toward their shores.

A Norse Ship of the Tenth Century
The remains of this ship were found in 1880.

Even France learned to dread the daring ventures of these Northmen or Vikings. There seemed no limit to what they would attempt. One of their leaders, called Rollo, forced from the French king a province on the northern coast of France. Rollo named it Normandy, and his descendants have lived there ever since.

Nor was France the only land which the Northmen molested. Even before Rollo seized his French province, his countrymen had raided the English coast. But these Vikings were not so lucky as Rollo. Although they conquered large districts north of the Thames River, they were soon driven away by England's good King Alfred.

And, strange as it may seem, these bold sailors were the first white men to visit the coasts of the great continent which lay across the sea, as yet undreamed of by any European race.

It happened in this way. Out to the west of the Northmen's land lay the island of Iceland. Here the Northmen planted a flourishing colony of happy, prosperous people. And here dwelt Eric the Red and his family.

This Eric the Red was as brave and fierce a warrior as ever lived, with a temper hard to control. Once upon a time he fell out with a neighbor, and in his anger killed the man. Such actions would not do, even in the Northmen's republic; so Eric the Red was banished from Iceland, as was just and right.

Soon a little Norse ship was plowing the angry waves of the Atlantic Ocean under the command of the exiled Eric. He was determined to seek his fortune in some new land, and daringly headed his vessel for the west, not knowing what lay before him.

Finally one day the outlines of a rough, forbidding coast came in sight. "This country, bleak as it is, may answer our purpose," reasoned Eric. So for three years he and his followers explored the shores of the land they had found.

At last they chose the pleasantest place they had seen, and there decided to make their home. Eric the Red named the new country Greenland; for, as he wisely said, "It is well to give it a pleasing name, you know, if we want others to be tempted to join us here."

This was just what Eric did want. He wanted to found a colony in Greenland. So he returned to Iceland and told the people wonderful tales about the beautiful land he had discovered. His stories so appealed to the adventurous spirit of his people that, when he set sail from Iceland the second time, twenty-five ships were needed to carry the colonists who went with him. Sad to say, eleven of the twenty-five ships were lost on the way. The other fourteen reached Greenland in safety, and the new colonists went busily to work building themselves homes.

The Ruins of a Church Built by the Northmen in Greenland

Among Eric's colonists there was a certain man who had a devoted but roving son, named Biarni. After having made a long voyage this son went back to Iceland, full of enthusiasm in the thought of seeing his father again. Picture his disappointment on reaching his old home and being told that his father had moved to the new colony in Greenland!

But Biarni was not to be cheated out of his great desire and at once set sail for Greenland. He had scarcely left Iceland when a terrible storm arose, and the winds blew his vessel toward the south. For days and days he sailed on without knowing where he was. Then he came in sight of a thickly wooded land very different from what he had heard Greenland to be. His sailors wished to go ashore, but Biarni said, "No, I shall not rest until I have seen my father, who is with Eric the Red."

So they turned the ship northward and sailed until at last they reached Greenland. Little did Biarni suspect that he had seen a new world!

Biarni naturally talked of the strange lands he had seen on his trip to Greenland. He told the colonists about them; and later, when he went to Norway, he told about them there.

What Biarni reported in Norway of these lands reached the ears of Eric the Red's eldest son, Leif, who lived in Norway at the time. Leif found Biarni's tales so interesting that he determined to go himself to see the new country.

First, Leif went to Greenland and there made ready for his voyage of discovery. Then he and his sailors set sail for the south. Many days passed before they saw land. Early one morning the eager cry of "Land! land!" was raised; and great was the excitement when they saw before them a low, sandy coast covered with fine forests.

"This land shall be called Markland," said Leif. "It must be the land that Biarni saw. Let us go ashore."

The Northmen did not remain any length of time in Markland, but sailed on till they came to a river that flowed into a channel. They sailed slowly up the river and soon came to a lake. Here they cast anchor. Some of the men went ashore and explored the new-found region. Everything seemed so charming that they decided to put up wooden huts and to spend the winter in them.

Explorations were cautiously made, but no inhabitants were to be seen. One night one of the men who had wandered off failed to come back. A party was sent out to find him. They became more and more anxious. After searching a long time, they came upon their lost comrade; and to their surprise, he was in a state of happy excitement.

Monument to Leif Ericson in Boston, Massachusetts

Where had he been and what had happened? Everyone wanted to know. The man replied that he had been for a ramble and, wonderful to tell, had discovered countless vines loaded with grapes; and if the others had been

Leif the Lucky Discovers a New Land

Germans, as he was, and had been brought up in the land of luscious grapes, they would understand his joy.

The Northmen had never seen or tasted grapes before, but you can imagine that they soon shared with the German sailor his love for them. On account of the vines, Leif named the land Vinland.

All this was in the year 1000. When the next spring came, the Northmen went home to Greenland, their ship filled with timber and dried grapes. Leif received the name of "The Lucky," and after his father's death became head of the colony in Greenland.

Thorvald and Karlsefin

THE voyage of Leif the Lucky greatly impressed the Greenland colonists. So much so, in fact, that Leif's brother, Thorvald, became very enthusiastic over the wonders of Vinland; and in the year 1002 he and thirty companions set sail in Leif's ship.

They soon arrived at Vinland and, finding Leif's huts, spent two winters there. Early in the second spring they sailed farther south. In coasting thus, the explorers came upon a beautiful land covered with woods. All went ashore. On seeing how attractive the place was, Thorvald said, "I should like to build myself a home here."

Up to this time the Northmen had met no inhabitants; but, as they were wandering along the sands, they came upon three canoes turned bottom upward. They lifted these. Hidden under each canoe was a man. The Northmen killed two of the men, but the third escaped. Then being weary, Thorvald and his companions foolishly lay on the beach and went to sleep.

Suddenly, and without warning, one of his men cried out, "Arise, Thorvald! Tarry no longer, but haste to your ship! Arise, Thorvald!"

The men sprang to their feet and saw the woods alive with fierce natives who had come to avenge the death of their comrades. The Northmen ran to their boats and rowed swiftly to the ship. A few well-aimed arrows sent the natives fleeing.

But a sad thing had happened. A swift arrow had struck Thorvald and wounded him mortally. All the men gathered sorrowfully around their chief. Realizing that he was dying, Thorvald said to them, "Bury me here on these shores, the place where I have said I should like to build myself a home. Return to Greenland." They buried him as he had directed, and placed two crosses on his grave. Then they went back to Greenland with their sad tale.

Not long after Thorvald's death, there came to Greenland from Iceland a handsome, wealthy, and most energetic young man. His name was Karlsefin. He married a beautiful young woman; and together they hit upon the plan of trying to found a colony in Vinland. Others gladly promised to go with them; and in the spring the expedition set sail with all that was necessary to start their colony, even to the cattle to supply milk.

In due time the colonists reached Vinland, and there still stood Leif's huts to offer them a shelter. A little fishing and hunting showed that fish and game were plentiful, and that it would be easy enough to get food in their new home.

For a year the settlers had things their own way. Then the natives began to pay them visits. Of course these natives were really what we call Indians, but the colonists called them Skraelings, meaning "inferior people."

The first time the Skraelings came was early one morning. Some of the Northmen saw them approaching in canoes. They were ugly-looking men, with coarse, unkempt black hair and black eyes. They looked in wonder at the tall blond Northmen, and after a while paddled away. For several months nothing more was seen of these strange visitors.

Then suddenly one day a great number of natives appeared in their canoes. They had come to trade with the Northmen. They proved to be especially fond of the red cloth that the Northmen had. In exchange for it the Skraelings gave skins of animals.

The Skraelings continued to come in such great numbers that the Northmen were soon short of red cloth, so Karlsefin divided what they had into narrow strips. Some were not more than an inch in width, but the natives gave as much for these narrow strips as they had given for the wider.

After a while something happened which changed this peaceful relation between the Northmen and the

Skraelings. Karlsefin had a bull. Now, it is difficult to see how a bull could bring on a war, but that is what this bull did. Once when the Indians were trading with the settlers, it ran, loudly bellowing, out of the field in which it had been kept. Terribly frightened, the natives fled to their canoes.

For fully three weeks they were not seen. When they did appear, there was no more peace for the settlers. Quarrel after quarrel with the savage Indians kept them in constant terror. They never knew when to look for an attack. At last, after many of his brave men had been killed in these fights with the Skraelings, Karlsefin decided to give up his colony and go back to Greenland.

When the disappointed settlers sailed away from Vinland, just ten years had gone by since Leif's discovery of this beautiful country—his land of grapes, which most likely lay somewhere on the New England coast.

Still later, other expeditions came to its shores; but before long the Norsemen lost their interest in the new world. All trace of the white man's visits gradually faded away, and once more the Skraelings held full sway.

II

MARCO POLO

The Adventures of Nicolo and Maffeo Polo

OF course this round world of ours has not grown any larger or any smaller in the last seven hundred years. What really has grown very much in that time is the amount known about it.

In the year 1200, two hundred years after Leif Ericson had explored one little part of the earth, the people of Eastern Europe really knew very little about geography. They believed, however, that they knew all there was to know. They felt sure that the earth was a great square. On the four sides of the square anyone could see the four blue walls of sky. And resting on the four blue walls were the heavens where dwelt God and His angels. The lands that they knew formed the center of the square. On the west the lands ended in water. On the east lay Cathay, and about Cathay the people of Eastern Europe knew nothing. They thought of it as a great bog or swamp, full of dreadful beasts, hobgoblins, bugaboos, and monsters, which roamed about howling in a way to make one's hair fairly stand on end. And so it is no wonder that few of these people ventured into Cathay.

Now just as they were all wrong about the shape of the earth, so they were all wrong about Cathay. What they called Cathay, we call China; and in 1200 China was no more a swamp than it is to-day.

A mighty people lived in China, and they had a mighty empire and a mighty ruler. Their lands were rich in mines of coal and gold; ebony, bamboo, corn, silk, and spices were plentiful; and game of many sorts made hunting a favorite pastime. The subjects of the mighty Emperor journeyed in all directions, extending his power on every side by conquering the lands they visited.

While the Chinese Empire was thus spreading out north, east, south, and west, the merchants of Italy began, during the thirteenth century, to work gradually farther and farther east in order to increase their commerce.

In 1260 two merchant brothers of Venice, named Nicolo and Maffeo Polo, started on an eastern journey. To travel through the East, or even around the world, takes only a few weeks or months in this twentieth century. But in the thirteenth century traveling was a very different matter. There were no ships better than those of the Northmen, and a railroad was undreamed of. To journey by sea meant to be at the mercy of winds and tides, with no compass. To journey by land, one must go on foot or ride a mule or a horse.

So when the Polo brothers left home they said good-by for a long time—how long no one could tell. They were not bound for any particular point. They merely traveled on and on, making money by trading, seeing new and interesting sights, and still not coming to even the edge of the dreadful swamp which was supposed to lie to the east. They went so far that at last they found themselves before the very palace gates of the Emperor of China.

In those days the Chinese were willing and anxious to learn, and their doors were open to all who might come. The Emperor, whose name was Kublai Khan, was a wise and good ruler. He had never seen any Europeans before, and he welcomed Nicolo and Maffeo Polo to his court with great honor and was delighted to hear all they could tell him. He questioned them about their rulers, how they lived, how they fought. He asked the brothers all about their religion, about the Pope and about Rome. And as Nicolo and Maffeo told him all these things, he grew so interested that he wanted to have his subjects learn about the Christian faith.

Accordingly he urged the two Polos to go back to their own country, carrying a letter from him to the Pope. This letter begged that the Pope would send Kublai Khan one hundred Christians who could teach their faith to his people. One of the Emperor's barons was to go with the Polo brothers. The two merchants willingly undertook the mission and promised to obey all the Emperor's commands.

When they were ready to leave the palace, the Emperor gave them a Tablet of Authority. This was a tablet made of gold, such as was carried by the Emperor's army officers or messengers. On it was engraved Kublai

Map Showing the Countries Crossed by the Polo Family

Kublai Khan

Khan's order to supply them with all they might need
in any country they were crossing.

On the long journey home all went well with Nicolo
and Maffeo Polo, but the Chinese baron was taken ill
and had to be left behind.

In 1269 the two merchants reached Italy, only to
find that the Pope was dead. They could not deliver
Kublai Khan's letter until a new pope was elected; so,
while they waited, they went home to Venice to see
their families.

Nicolo's wife, too, had died while he was away,
leaving their son, Marco Polo, a boy fifteen years old.
For two years Maffeo and Nicolo stayed in Venice with
the boy. Then, a new pope being elected, they set out
once more on their travels. And this time they took
young Marco with them.

Marco Polo in China

FIRST the Polos went to Rome to see the new Pope. But although he was very gracious and willing to oblige Kublai Khan, he could furnish only two friars instead of the one hundred asked for as teachers. And these two at the last moment were so frightened at the idea of going into Cathay that they would not start.

In the fall of 1271, without a single friar, Nicolo, Maffeo, and Marco Polo and a few followers left Italy to carry the Pope's answer to Kublai Khan.

They crossed Turkey and came to the city of Bagdad. From Bagdad they went on to Persia. They had to be well armed as they traveled along, for in certain parts of Persia the people were very cruel and savage. They would stop at nothing, and often killed a whole party of merchants simply to get their wares.

At length the travelers reached a great plain where the heat was intense. Here and there they came upon a village surrounded by high walls of mud, built to shut out the bands of robbers which were a terror to the whole region.

Now these robbers were supposed to be able to bring such darkness over the plain that men riding side by side could hardly see each other. Then in this darkness the robbers would form long lines of many hundreds of men abreast and ride out over the plain. No one could see them coming, and whoever might be traveling on that part of the plain would be pretty sure to run into the lines and be taken.

Once Marco Polo himself was all but caught in this manner, but he got away and rushed to a nearby village. Only seven others of his party escaped. All the rest were caught and either sold for slaves or put to death.

Marco Polo

Marco fully believed the robbers had the power to bring about the dreaded darkness. What really happened were dust storms. The dust of the great plain would rise so thick that no one could see through it. And the robbers, knowing the plains so well that they had no fear of being lost, used the storms to serve their wicked purposes.

Out of the heat of the plain the travelers rode on day after day until they came, after much climbing, to the

Pamir Plateau. This plateau was so high that the people of that country named it "The Roof of the World." Here it was as cold as the plain was hot. Twelve days' riding was needed to cross the plateau, and during all that time the travelers had only what food they had brought with them. It was so cold that no people lived here, nothing green could grow, and even no birds were seen.

When Nicolo, Maffeo, Marco, and their followers reached the city of Lob, they stopped for a week's rest. And well they might, for ahead of them lay the great sandy desert of Gobi. It would take a month to ride over even the small part of it which they must cross. All their supplies must be carried, as they could expect nothing from the desert except here and there fresh water from a spring.

The journey was much to be dreaded, for the desert was believed to be haunted. Spirits were supposed to be on the watch for any traveler who might fall behind his party. If one of the party loitered, the spirits would call to him, making him think he heard the voice of his friends, but really leading him off to die alone. The voices were in truth nothing but the blowing of the winds across the sands. But in the silence of the desert and in the fear of being lost, it is no wonder that travelers often fancied themselves called, and rushed off toward the sounds. However, by keeping close together, by tying bells on the necks of their horses, and by putting up a sign at night to show which way they must go in the morning, the Polos crossed the desert in safety.

Finally, after having been nearly four years on the

way, they reached Kaipingfu or the City of Peace. Here was the beautiful cane palace where the Emperor spent the summer months, and here the travelers now found the great Kublai Khan.

Kneeling before him, they addressed him with all respect and gave him the letter from the Pope, which said that, although the Polos had not succeeded in doing all that the Emperor wished, still they had faithfully done their best. Kublai Khan was much pleased to see Nicolo and Maffeo again and gave them a cordial welcome. Then, noticing Marco, he asked, "Who is this with you?"

"Sire, this is my son and your liegeman," promptly answered Nicolo.

"Welcome is he too," graciously replied the Emperor. And from that time he took a lively interest in the young man.

At once Marco set himself to learn all he could in this new land. He was soon able to speak several languages, and he quickly came to understand the customs and manners of the Chinese court.

Oftentimes Marco was with the Emperor when some ambassador to a distant province reached home, and nearly always the ambassador would report on just what he had been sent to do and no more. When the Emperor would ask questions about other matters, he would learn little. Then he would say, "I had far rather hear about the strange things and manners of the different countries you have seen than merely to be told of the business you went upon."

Marco Polo remembered this point; and when the Emperor began sending him as ambassador to various parts of the kingdom, he took pains to notice all that was new and strange. On his return, therefore, he could tell Kublai Khan much that was interesting and valuable which he had either seen or learned by asking questions.

He told of a queer way in which bamboo was used in Tibet. He said: "In this region you find quantities of canes, full three palms in girth and fifteen paces in length, with some three palms interval between the joints. And let me tell you that merchants and other travelers are wont at nightfall to gather these canes and make fires of them; for as they burn they make such loud reports that the lions and bears and other wild beasts are greatly frightened and make off as fast as possible—in fact, nothing will induce them to come near a fire of that sort. . . . In fact, but for the help of these canes, which make such a noise in burning that the beasts are terrified and kept at a distance, no one would be able even to travel through the land."

In another province Marco saw crocodiles for the first time. He called them "great serpents" and told of their huge mouths, large enough to swallow a man whole, and of the terrible fear the people had of them.

In still another province Marco found that the men had their teeth covered with cases of gold, which they took off when they ate; and that their arms were tattooed in broad black bands. Excepting in time of war these men did nothing but hunt and take their ease, leaving all the work to their wives and slaves.

Although he never visited Japan, young Polo was much impressed with all he heard about the vast amount of gold, the great number of pearls, the fine woods, and the spices to be found in that empire. Indeed, so glowing were the tales he repeated of these riches, as well as of the diamonds of India, that the reports were never forgotten. After centuries they still influenced explorers looking for wealth.

Year after year Marco Polo, his father, and uncle lived in China. While Marco served the Emperor, the other two gathered riches in various ways. Often they longed to return to their own country, but whenever they talked of leaving, Kublai Khan urged them not to go. However, when they had been in his court for seventeen years, their chance came.

The Khan of Persia was a great nephew to Kublai Khan. He wanted a wife and asked the Chinese Emperor to send him one. A beautiful girl of seventeen was chosen to be his bride. But then came the question of how to get her to Persia. Wars which were being carried on made it unsafe to go by land, and the Chinese were not great sailors. Therefore, when the three Venetians offered to take the little bride by sea, Kublai Khan could not say no.

In 1292 they sailed away from China. The voyage was so stormy that they did not reach the Persian Gulf for twenty-six months, and by that time the Khan who had sent for a wife had died. What became of the poor little princess? She was married offhand to the old Khan's son.

Marco Polo's Return to Venice—His Book

ONE day in the year 1295 the people of Venice were surprised to see coming into their city three wayworn travelers. The strangers were dressed in rather shabby and very queerly cut clothes, and judging from their manner and accent, they came from far away. Who were they and what could they want in Venice?

The Return of the Polo Family to Venice

On they went until they came to the beautiful house which belonged to the ancient family of Polo. Here they stated that they were members of that family and had come home to live. They said that they were Nicolo, Maffeo, and Marco Polo just returning from Cathay. This seemed hardly probable. To be sure many years ago two robust men and a boy, all named Polo, had gone off to that unknown country, but they had been given up for lost long since. Two of these men were old and wrinkled, and the youngest was forty-one. Was it possible that they could have lived twenty-four years in a land supposed to be so terrible?

In some way the strangers convinced their family that they were really Marco, his father, and his uncle; and they were allowed to take possession of their old home.

Still there were friends who doubted. So, to settle these questions for good and all, they invited these friends to a banquet. Everything was of the finest, and the guests were deeply impressed. But when the last course had been served and the servants had left the room, a wonderful sight was in store for them. Marco left the table, went into another room for a moment, and came back carrying the shabby coats which he, Nicolo, and Maffeo had worn on their return to Venice. With sharp knives the three began ripping up the seams. Out rolled rubies, diamonds, emeralds, carbuncles, and sapphires, until the table was covered with so many treasures that no one could even guess at their value. Seeing such wealth the guests were easily convinced that their hosts must indeed have been in the service of the great Emperor they told about.

The story of the dinner and the jewels spread rapidly. Soon all the Venetians flocked to see the great travelers, to pay them every respect, and to hear from them tales of the wonders of the East. Some of these were believed, but many were not, simply because they seemed too unreal to be true.

In the thirteenth century the city of Venice was a republic. So was the city of Genoa. The two republics were deadly rivals and were almost constantly at war with each other. In the year 1298 there was a great naval battle between the two, and Marco Polo was the commander of a powerful galley for the Venetians. The Genoese won the battle and took seven thousand prisoners, one of whom was Marco.

For a year he was imprisoned in Genoa. When he was released he went back to Venice. There he lived for twenty-five years, and there he died in 1324.

But to return to the year Marco Polo spent in the prison in Genoa. This was in truth a most important period of his life. Shut up in the prison with him was a man named Rusticiano. He and Marco became friends; and, to while away the time, Marco told Rusticiano of his adventures in the East. It happened that Rusticiano knew how to write—a rare accomplishment at that time. He was deeply interested in all Marco had to tell of his wonderful travels, and offered to write them in book form. So Marco began over again at the beginning, and as he told the story Rusticiano patiently wrote down all he said.

As there were no printing presses in those days, the

Marco Polo Dictating an Account of His Voyages

book when finished had all been done by hand. But that was not the remarkable part of it. Its great value lay in the fact that it carefully described for the first time a route which had actually been traveled across the entire length of Asia. Here were true stories of the great Chinese Empire, of the wealth of all the Eastern provinces; and, most important of all perhaps, here was the account of a journey taken on a great ocean which lay even beyond those Eastern provinces.

The people of Marco Polo's own time could not make themselves believe all his tales. But in the centuries

26

which followed, the influence of his book was very great.

Years afterwards wise men came gradually to understand that the earth is round. And from this knowledge grew the belief that the ocean to the west of Europe and Marco's ocean to the east of China were all one. So, perhaps for the reason that he was the first to describe the Eastern sea, much credit is due directly to Marco Polo that, sailing west to reach India, two hundred years later, Columbus discovered the American continent.

III

CHRISTOPHER COLUMBUS

His Plan

FROM the days of Marco Polo commerce between the East and the Italian cities grew and flourished. The republics of Genoa and Venice were among the most important of the trade centers.

Genoa sent her cargoes of copper, iron, hides, and wool to India by way of Constantinople and the Black and Caspian seas. Venice sent her vessels by way of Alexandria and the Red Sea.

Neither of these routes was without serious drawbacks. The Venetian ships could go only as far as Alexandria, for the Suez Canal had not yet been made. Then the merchants had to unload, transport their wares across the isthmus, and reship them on the Red Sea. The Genoese had the same trouble in traveling by way of Constantinople. At some point on the Black Sea their goods were taken from the ships and loaded on caravans; then, after braving all the dangers of the sea, the merchants had to face the greater dangers of overland travel. One never knew when a caravan might be overhauled by bandits and all the valuable wares stolen. The merchants were lucky who escaped with their lives from such attacks.

Nor did the strain of these voyages end with reaching India. There the ships and caravans were loaded for the home trip with the riches of that land. And surely the costly diamonds, pearls, ivory, silks and spices of the East could not fail to tempt robbers and pirates as much as did the Italian products.

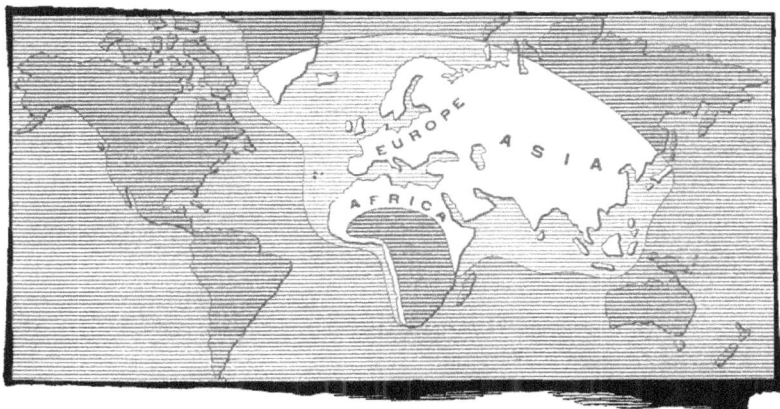

The Part of the World Known at the Time
Columbus Sailed for China (shown in white)

So it was no easy matter at best for Genoa to trade with India. Still, encouraged by those who succeeded, and trying to forget those who came to grief, the Genoese merchants went back and forth until the middle of the fifteenth century.

Then suddenly their trade route was cut off. Constantinople was captured by the Turks, and the Turks would not allow ships from Genoa to sail into the Black Sea. It was a dreadful blow to the prosperity of the republic. Some new course must be found. But where and by whom?

When this disaster befell Genoa the same questions were continually being asked in other lands than Italy. Portugal was among the most eager of the seekers for a new route to the East. Her hope was to find a passage around the southern part of Africa; and year after year she sent her ships farther and farther down the western coast of that continent searching for a southern passage.

From time to time on such voyages there was to be seen among the Portuguese sailors a tall, handsome, ruddy young seaman with long flowing hair and commanding blue-gray eyes. Christopher Columbus he was called.

Columbus was born in Genoa, probably about the year 1436. He was the son of a wool comber. Until his tenth year Christopher helped his father in his trade. Then he spent four years in the University of Pavia, learning mathematics, reading, writing, and the laws of navigation.

On leaving Pavia he was sent by his father to sea. For some time he sailed up and down the Mediterranean in merchant vessels. But later he went to Portugal, and from there sailed, not only far south along the shores of Africa, but also north even as far as Iceland.

You must remember, however, that a sailor's lot was very different then from what it is now. The Europeans of the fifteenth century had only sailing vessels, and not very large or very strongly built ones at that. As their speed depended entirely upon the strength of the wind, no one could foretell how long any voyage might take.

To be sure, by the time Columbus sailed the seas the compass had come into use. This compass consisted of a magnetized steel bar or needle resting on a pivot. North of the equator the head of a magnetic needle always turns to the north. So no matter how far out on the ocean sailors might be, they could tell at any time which way to turn to get home.

Then, too, the explorers had maps of the world. But many of the maps at that time were very queer and had

The Earliest Engraved Portrait of Christopher Columbus

pictures of dreadful sea serpents and horrible monsters drawn between the countless little islands.

This was due to the stories told by sailors, who were very superstitious. In the dark nights when they were out upon the sea, they would imagine all sorts of creatures moving in the darkness beyond. The spray thrown up by the ship would look like mermaids with great glistening eyes who beckoned them to come to their home in the deep. These stories were fully believed, and wherever a sailor had seen such sights they were put down on the map.

The great trouble was that very few people knew the real facts. Most of them still thought that the earth was a flat surface, surrounded on all sides by a large ocean.

A very few learned men thought differently. These few said that the earth was round, as we know it to be. But even they made mistakes. They believed the world to be much smaller than it really is. They knew nothing about America, and thought that only one ocean—the Atlantic—separated Europe from India and China.

Columbus, after paying close attention to all he could see or hear of such matters on his many trips, came to think the same as the wise men; and this belief opened big possibilities to him. Born in Genoa and sailing under the flag of Portugal, is it any wonder that he was easily fired with the desire to find a route to India as yet untried by anyone? Plans began to form in his mind and fairly to take possession of him.

Once when he was visiting the Azores the inhabitants showed him some bits of curiously carved wood and branches of unknown trees that had been driven ashore by the Western seas. They also told him of two drowned men the waves had washed up, whose appearance was altogether different from any European's. Such things could have come only from a country to the west, reasoned Columbus. And the stories confirmed him still further in his growing belief that to sail west was the way to reach India.

Finally he wrote to a noted astronomer of Florence,

Toscanelli's Map (restored and simplified)

named Toscanelli, and asked his advice. Marco Polo's stories of the wealth of China and Japan, and above all what Marco Polo had written about a sea to the east of these lands, had so influenced this Toscanelli that he too had tried to plan some way of reaching them. His plans and those of Columbus proved to be the same. When he answered Columbus's letter he sent with his reply a map of the world made by himself and showing the course that he believed would lead to China.

But like the maps of the other learned men, Toscanelli's map showed only three continents—Europe, Asia, and Africa. Where America lies he drew China and Japan. And he too made the distance much too short.

As a rule, of course, mistakes do much harm. However these mistakes of Toscanelli's turned out to be an exception. Bent as he was on reaching China, do you suppose that Columbus would ever have sailed west if he had suspected for a moment that a great continent lay between him and that country?

Some people think that when Columbus visited Iceland he must have heard of the discovery of Vinland. But if he did hear of such a land he could never have understood where it was. He accepted Toscanelli's map as accurate and longed to test this plan of sailing directly west to China.

But Columbus was poor and had not the money to carry out his enterprise. Where could he turn for help? First he tried Genoa and Venice. The people only laughed at his wild plans. They thought he must be mad.

Columbus Describing His Plan for Reaching China
(from the painting by Sir David Wilkie)

Then he went to Portugal. But neither would the Portuguese listen to him. Instead they ridiculed him and asked whether he really believed that the earth was round and that people on the other side walked with their heads down.

In spite of all this opposition Columbus was not discouraged. He now went to Spain where King Ferdinand and Queen Isabella reigned. For seven long years Columbus stayed there trying to persuade the King and Queen to give him ships to cross the ocean. At last Queen Isabella consented to furnish the necessary money and promised to pawn her own jewels if Spain could not give him enough.

The First Voyage

On the 3d of August, 1492, Columbus left the port of Palos with three vessels, the *Pinta*, the *Niña* and the *Santa Maria*. This last was the flagship, and was the only one with an entire deck. Although the largest of the fleet, the *Santa Maria* was not over ninety feet long and twenty feet wide.

It had been no easy task to find men to man these ships. When the most learned men were unwilling to aid Columbus, what could be expected of poor ignorant sailors? In order to get men to manage the ships, convicts were taken out of jail and promised their liberty if they would go with Columbus. Others were forced to go by the King.

The vessels arrived at the Canary Islands the 12th of August and stayed there three weeks, as the *Pinta* needed repairs.

When they were again out upon the sea and could see no land, the fears of the sailors rose. What horrible monsters would they meet? What if they should fall off the edge of the earth! What if this wind that carried them on so swiftly should prevent their going home!

As the weeks passed and no land appeared, a mutiny threatened to break out. But Columbus, noticing this restlessness and growing fear among the men, encouraged them from day to day with new hope.

After a few weeks they came into a region where the air was soft and balmy. Queer objects were floating out to meet them—sticks carved with strange figures, and once a branch of berries. Now the men were very happy, and all kept a diligent lookout for land.

One evening a sailor spied something dark against the horizon. "Land!" he shouted. When morning came, there, stretched before them, was the New World. Red-skinned natives were running excitedly up and down the shores wondering who these strange white people were.

*Columbus Claiming the New Country
in the Name of Spain*

This was the 12th of October, 1492. The crew went ashore and, falling on their knees, kissed the ground in their great joy. With much ceremony Columbus unfurled the banner he had brought with him and took possession of the country in the name of Spain. He gave the island the name of San Salvador.

"This island must be a little north of Japan," thought Columbus. It was a beautiful spot; but there were certainly no traces of the great palace with the golden roof, of the courtiers of the king laden down with silk and precious jewels, or of the busy wharves crowded with vessels, which Columbus had expected to see when he touched the shores of Japan. Evidently he must sail a little farther before he could see these wonders or deliver the letter he carried from Ferdinand and Isabella to the Khan of China.

Cruising about, still looking for Japan or the coast of China, Columbus discovered the islands of Cuba and Haiti. To the whole group he gave the name West Indies, and so naturally he called the natives Indians.

Early Christmas morning, before it was light, a cry went up from the deck of the *Santa Maria*. The flagship had struck on a sand bar just off the coast of Haiti. All efforts to set her free were useless. Soon the waves had broken to pieces the best and largest of Columbus's little fleet.

What if another such accident should happen, and there should be no way to send word back to Spain that he had at least reached the islands near Japan and China! Frightened by this thought, Columbus determined to sail for home. With the largest ship gone, all the sailors could not now be carried. So forty men were left in Haiti, when their commander sailed for Spain.

On the 15th of March Columbus arrived in Palos. As soon as he landed he sent to the Royal Treasurer of Spain a letter in which he told all about his discoveries.

News of Columbus's good fortune soon spread all over Spain and Portugal. Everybody was eager to welcome the great man. They forgot all the mean things they had said about him and were ready to praise him for what he had done.

You can imagine how the King and Queen felt when Columbus presented himself at their court. He told them all about the New World and what he had seen there. He showed them all the curious things he had brought—the wonderful birds, unknown fruits, and, above all, several natives from the new country. Columbus was recognized as a hero. The King gave him the title of "Don" and treated him almost as an equal.

But the great honors lavished upon the successful admiral soon made enemies for him among the jealous courtiers. One day at a dinner given in his honor Columbus was telling about his voyage. Another guest remarked that he did not think there was anything so very wonderful about discovering the West Indies. With quiet dignity Columbus took an egg and, turning to the man, asked, "Can you stand this egg on end?"

Why, no, he couldn't; and neither could any other guest at the table, although they all tried.

When the egg was handed back to Columbus he struck it lightly on the table, cracking the shell just enough to make it stand upright. Then everyone laughed to see how easily it could be done.

"Just so easily anyone could have discovered the West Indies after I had shown the way," said Columbus.

Other Voyages

WHEN in September, 1493, Columbus sailed upon his second voyage, he had no difficulty in getting sailors. Everybody was eager to see the new land and share in its riches. The fleet consisted of seventeen vessels and fifteen hundred men.

This time Columbus landed on the island of Porto Rico. But when the people found no gold lying around, they began to murmur and criticise their leader. Columbus, as always, told them to hope and wait.

When he went back to Spain after nearly three years, most of the men who had come with him stayed on the islands. Columbus still believed he was near the coast of Japan or China, and never during his lifetime did he know that he was the discoverer of America.

But now no royal welcome was given the returning explorer. You see that even from his second trip he had brought back no gold and none of the wealth of the East; and that is what the Spanish people wanted. He was an upstart and a fraud.

However, as Queen Isabella still believed in him

and encouraged him, Columbus fitted out six vessels and in 1498 started on his third voyage. This time he sailed farther south and discovered the Orinoco River.

Leaving the Orinoco River, Columbus cruised to the West Indies. There the colonists had turned against him, and when he came among them they put him in chains and sent him back to Spain. Columbus wore his chains with dignity and patience. But when he reached Spain the Queen was so indignant at his treatment that he was immediately released.

In 1502 Columbus made one more voyage. Again he returned without having reached the Chinese Empire and with no gold. Isabella soon died, and the King took no more notice of the great man.

Columbus was now an old man, his health was broken, and he was very poor. In 1506 he died. He had discovered a new world, and all the thanks he received was to be ignored.

Through his efforts, Spain became one of the wealthiest and strongest countries in Europe. She founded great colonies across the ocean, which carried on a wonderful trade with the Old World.

And not Spain alone, but all Europe, profited indirectly by the discoveries of Columbus. Even before his death different nations began sending out explorers to plant their banners on any lands they might find and thus to extend their power in the New World to the west.

You would suppose that our continent would have been named after Columbus. Instead it was called

America after a certain Florentine adventurer, Americus Vespucius, who crossed the ocean after Columbus, and who wrote a book about his travels.

IV

JOHN CABOT

CONSIDERING how slowly news generally traveled from country to country in the time of Columbus, the report of his first voyage seems to have spread with wonderful rapidity. Before long England knew all about it, and the English king was saying to himself, "If Spain has really sent ships to the west and reached these islands off the coast of China, why can't England do the same? And why can't we have some of the wealth of China and Japan? I will see that we do have, and I will see that the English flag is planted in this distant land."

Now England always wanted, and took measures to get, her full share of whatever offered itself. Still in this instance Henry VII probably acted more promptly than he otherwise would have, because he felt that he had at hand just the right man to help him out.

This man was John Cabot, and he too was full of enthusiasm over the possibilities of a western voyage.

Cabot was born in 1450, probably in Genoa. He moved to Venice while still young, and later became a citizen of that city. To become a citizen of Venice he had to reside there fifteen years, and during that time he made his living by drawing maps and charts. In 1490 he and his wife left Venice and settled in Bristol, which was at that time the chief seaport of England, and the center of trade with the fisheries of Iceland.

Cabot was soon a great favorite with King Henry; and seeing the King's interest in the voyage of Columbus, he added to it by telling things about China learned from the merchants of Venice. Then Cabot suggested that, if King Henry would fit out a ship to cross the Atlantic, he would gladly sail in command of such an expedition.

So it was agreed; and in May, 1497, John Cabot, and in all probability his son Sebastian, with one vessel and eighteen men set sail from Bristol. On the 24th of June the coast of Labrador was sighted. Where they landed is not definitely known, but probably it was near the island of Cape Breton.

This cold, bleak land was very different from the China they had expected to see. They had hoped to find a land of spicy groves and balmy breezes, but here was a land of snow and icebergs. Most of John Cabot's papers and maps telling of this voyage were lost; but some of them have been kept, and they tell about this cold region with its white bears, and about the great number of codfish that were seen and caught.

Cabot planted the flag of England and took possession of the land in the name of the English king. This planting of the English flag laid the foundation for the English claims in the new continent.

Cabot and His Ship Leaving Labrador

Great was the rejoicing when Cabot returned to England with the tale of his discoveries. The people of Bristol were extremely proud of their "Great Admiral," as he was now called. Whenever he walked the streets, dressed in silks and velvets, great crowds would follow him. He was especially loved by children, who crowded round him to hear him tell of his wondrous voyage.

Sebastian Cabot
When an Old Man

In 1498 John Cabot determined to undertake another voyage, and in April of that year he and Sebastian sailed with five or six ships. They sailed much farther north in the hope of finding a short passage to India. But the extreme cold of the northern region "chilled their enthusiasm," as Sebastian said; so they turned and sailed south along the American coast.

In September of that year (1498) only one of the six ships returned to England; and it is feared that John Cabot and his ship were lost, as nothing more was ever heard of the man who had first touched the mainland of North America since the days of Leif the Lucky.

V

THE SPANISH CONQUESTS
AND EXPLORATIONS

Ponce de Leon

THE discovery by Columbus of a supposed sea route to Asia aroused the Spaniards both young and old. Many, attracted by the hope of gold or the love of adventure, left Spain for the new land.

Colony after colony was planted in the West Indies. Colonial governors were appointed; and practically a new, but crude, Spain was established. Then, feeling that nothing was too great to attempt with the long sea voyage safely over, the boldest of the adventurers sailed away again, each bent upon finding what seemed to him most desirable.

One of these Spanish seekers was called Juan Ponce de Leon. He had come to the new land with Columbus on his second voyage and, remaining, had been made governor of Porto Rico. This was very fine, but the Governor had his own reasons for not being perfectly happy. He was growing old; and to enjoy this new life thoroughly, a man should have the vigor of youth.

47

If only he were young again! With this great wish in his heart, Ponce de Leon one day heard of an island on which was a marvelous fountain. Whoever should drink of the water of this fountain, no matter how old he was, would find himself young again. Here was just what Ponce de Leon wanted above all else. He determined to find the Fountain of Youth at any cost. The Spanish king gave him permission to go in search of the island and, if he found it, to become its governor for life.

So Ponce de Leon had three splendid ships built with his own money and, when they were completed, started on his travels. This was in 1513.

One day the sailors spied land. On approaching, they found it to be a glorious country, full of splendid groves and beautiful wild flowers growing in the tall grasses and along the low shores. And the singing of the birds among the branches sounded sweet indeed.

It was Easter Sunday, called by the church Pasqua Florida, or Flowery Easter; so, in honor of the day, and also because of the beautiful wild flowers, Ponce de Leon named the country Florida. He landed where St. Augustine now stands and took the land in the name of the King of Spain.

He explored the country for many miles along the coast. But beautiful as it was, its birds and wild flowers failed to tell him where to find the Fountain of Youth. So this poor knight had to sail back to Porto Rico, an older and wiser man than when he left.

In 1521 Ponce de Leon sailed again for his flower province to found a colony. But the natives were hostile.

When the Spaniards landed, a storm of poisoned arrows greeted them. Many of the soldiers were killed. Ponce de Leon himself was wounded. A few who managed to escape to their ships bore their leader with them. They sailed to Cuba, and there Ponce de Leon died—an old man still.

The Fountain of Youth has never been discovered.

Hernando Cortez

ONE day an exploring expedition which had sailed from Cuba returned to that island. The leader had startling news to tell. He and his men had been to Mexico and had found there many wondrous things. The country was ruled by the Aztecs—a race of Indians who worshiped the sun and moon and the god of war. Unlike the natives of the West Indies, the Mexican Indians had beautiful temples and palaces; and they boasted of the endless gold to be had in their country.

So gold had been found at last! Nothing more was needed to make Mexico seem an enchanted country to the greedy Spaniards.

No time was lost in getting ready a new expedition and in choosing for its leader a brave, daring young Spanish soldier named Hernando Cortez. Unlike Ponce de Leon, Cortez set out, not merely to follow a will-o'-the-wisp, but to make an actual conquest.

It was early in 1519 when Cortez sailed from Cuba. In March he reached Mexico and, after a sharp skirmish with the natives at Tabasco, skirted the coast until he came to the present site of Vera Cruz. There he set up a fortified camp. Then he sank his ships so that his men would be obliged to follow him, and prepared to march to the City of Mexico.

Ruins of an Ancient Aztec Palace

Now there was a tradition among the Aztecs that, many years before, a man had appeared who was of the race of the Children of the Sun. They called him the Wonderchild. He had golden hair and was as fair as day. He stayed with them several years and taught them many things. One day he told them that they would see him no more, but that the men of his race would soon come and conquer the land of the Aztecs. Then he disappeared and was never seen again.

So when Montezuma, the Aztec ruler, heard that the Spaniards were coming toward the City of Mexico, he was indeed frightened. These men must be the race of which the Wonderchild had spoken.

How could he stop their coming to take possession of his capital? Perhaps presents would do. In this hope Montezuma sent messengers with rich gifts of gold and gems to meet the Spaniards and to beg them to turn back. Cortez paid no attention to their entreaties. Instead, he marched on to the city, where Montezuma very graciously received him, thinking, most likely, to make a virtue of necessity. And here week after week the Spaniards stayed, honored guests of the Indian chief, living on the best the land afforded.

But Cortez was not contented to be a guest. He had come to conquer. He had only a handful of soldiers, and Montezuma had thousands at his command. It was a bad situation. Finally he decided to capture the ruler. So one day he invited Montezuma to an interview; and when he arrived at the palace

Hernando Cortez

occupied by the Spaniards, Cortez took him prisoner.

When the Aztecs heard of the fate of their chief they were hot with anger. Still they were afraid to attack the palace for fear of killing Montezuma, whom they worshiped almost as a god.

Just at this time Cortez left for the coast. It seems that the Spaniards in Cuba had become jealous of Cortez and had sent soldiers to bring him back. Hearing of the plan, Cortez with less than two hundred men made a forced march to their camp and surprised and conquered them. This done, he returned at once to the City of Mexico.

While he was gone the soldiers left in charge at the capital had attacked the natives at a festival and killed hundreds of them. Then the Mexicans had turned upon their foes and would have slaughtered all, had not Cortez returned just in time. In order to save his men Cortez commanded Montezuma to show himself to the people from the top of the palace. When the natives saw their beloved chief they were delighted. In a moment, however, they were angry again; for Montezuma asked them to make peace. This they refused to do. In the fight that followed, Montezuma received a wound from which he soon died.

After this battle the Spaniards were obliged to flee. Instead of leaving the country, however, they returned and besieged the city for months. At last, in August, 1521, the Aztecs surrendered their capital. Cortez took it in the name of the King of Spain. The superstition of the Aztecs, and the wonderful perseverance of Cortez had made his voyage a success, and Mexico a Spanish land.

Balboa and Pizarro

ONE day, several years before Mexico became a possession of Spain, there came to a certain Indian village on the Isthmus of Panama, a party of Spaniards. At their head marched Balboa, the commander of the Spanish-Panama settlement.

So great a guest must be received with all possible ceremony. The visitors were welcomed to the home of the chief himself, and every honor was showered upon them. The Spaniards, in turn, were on their best behavior. Cordial greetings, compliments, and expressions of lasting friendship filled the air.

Then the Indian chief was moved to show even more plainly his love for the white man. So he gave Balboa seventy slaves and much gold.

As if by magic all was confusion. The greedy Spaniards began to quarrel over the gold, and hot words put a sudden end to the pleasure of a moment before.

With offended dignity the Indians watched and listened. At last the chief's son rose and said, "Brothers, your actions lead us to think you set great value on this yellow stuff, since you quarrel over it. If this be true, why do you not go to the southland, on the shore of the great western sea, where there is more than enough for all?"

Why not, indeed? This simple question resulted in Balboa's going in search of the new sea, and in his being the first European to gaze on the waters of the largest ocean on the globe. Then, drawing his sword, the discoverer of the Pacific waded out knee-deep and, standing in the water, claimed it for Spain with all the lands that border it.

Balboa Claiming the Pacific Ocean and
Its Shores for the King of Spain

Balboa found the Pacific Ocean, but not the land of gold. The Indian boy's tale of such a country was not forgotten, however; and years later the honor of its conquest fell to the lot of Francisco Pizarro, a soldier in the Spanish settlement on Panama.

Fired by the success of Cortez, two of Pizarro's friends suggested that he go in search of the famed country to the south. They said that they would furnish the money if he would head the expedition. The only condition was that Pizarro divide the spoils of the conquest equally among the three. Pizarro was delighted.

In 1525 he started in search of the golden kingdom of Peru. He invaded the country of the Incas and found splendid cities filled with rich treasures and beautiful buildings and temples. The Incas were the royal race of Peru. Like the Aztecs they claimed to be descendants of the sun.

Pizarro had only a few warriors with him, so, although he wanted very much to conquer the country, he dared not attempt it at this time. He went to Spain. There he was received at court as a great future conqueror and had no difficulty in obtaining men and money for his expedition to Peru.

Francisco Pizarro

With his small army Pizarro realized that the only way to conquer the Peruvians would be to capture their Inca or chief. He sent one of his bravest men, Hernando de Soto, with some soldiers and requested the Inca to come to the Spanish camp. The Inca, whose name was Atahualpa, hesitated at first, but at last decided to go.

When he reached Pizarro's camp, he was subjected to a trick whereby that unscrupulous leader meant to entrap the poor Inca. After receiving him with great show of friendliness, Pizarro had a priest read the story of the Bible. As soon as the priest had ended, Pizarro commanded the Inca to embrace the Catholic faith. As Pizarro fully expected, Atahualpa refused. And using his refusal as an excuse, the Spaniards thrust him into prison.

Naturally Atahualpa was very anxious to get out; so in order to obtain his freedom, he promised the Spaniards a room filled with gold and gems. In a short time the Peruvians had filled the chamber with rich treasures. Still the Spaniards were not satisfied. A rumor was abroad that a large army was coming to rescue the Inca and destroy the Spaniards. This was a good excuse for these cruel foreigners. So they killed poor Atahualpa in spite of his pleadings for mercy.

When the natives heard of the horrible death of their ruler, they were justly indignant. Pizarro, however, managed to make peace with them and became lord of the land. Several times the natives tried to get rid of the hated white man, but they soon realized that it was useless.

Pizarro did not live long to enjoy his newly acquired wealth. While he was so busy in Peru he had almost forgotten his two friends, who had helped him to his success. One of them died during these years. The other,

Pizarro contrived to have killed because he rebelled against the small share of spoils that the conquerer gave him.

Now the murdered man had a son, and this son swore to avenge the death of his father. Pizarro heard of the plot and tried to escape, but the young man was not to be cheated. He followed his enemy to his very palace, and there he killed him. And so ended the career of Francisco Pizarro.

Hernando de Soto

NOT only had Pizarro become a wealthy man through the conquest of Peru, but so had every Spaniard who was with him. Hernando de Soto, the young Spanish soldier, was counted not only among the bravest, but also among the richest of these; and to him, in return for his services, Charles V of Spain gave the governorship of Cuba.

Hernando de Soto

Yet De Soto was not content. He wanted more gold. So in 1539 he fitted out an expedition and, taking six hundred men and two hundred horses, sailed west in the hope of finding a second Peru. The army landed on the eastern coast of Florida and began their march inland.

We have seen that the Spaniards were naturally very cruel. Nor did they intend to mend their ways on this trip, as is shown by the fact that they carried with them fetters to bind the captured, and bloodhounds to bring back runaway prisoners. The soldiers seized the poor natives, chained them in couples and, driving them like beasts, forced them to carry the baggage. If an Indian refused to act as guide or in any way disobeyed, his punishment was terrible. The least he could hope for was to have his hands chopped off. Death by torture was the common fate. It is no wonder that such treatment made the Indians hate the Spaniards and in turn lose no chance to do them harm.

Owing largely to this bitter feeling, De Soto's journey was full of dangers almost from the very start. He had hoped to find a country full of gold and had promised his soldiers great rewards. But they were doomed to disappointment. The Indians would tell them very little and, when forced to act as guides, would often lead them into some swamp and, slipping away, leave them to get out as best they could.

Two years were spent in making this tedious march across the States of Florida, Georgia, Alabama, and Mississippi. Still no quantity of gold was found, and still the brave but brutal leader would not turn back.

One spring day in 1541, the Spaniards, worn out and discouraged, were making their way through a dense forest. Suddenly through an opening in the trees they caught the blue gleam of a river. Hurrying to its banks De Soto beheld the mighty Mississippi, the Father of Waters. The object of his long search was gold; but had De Soto found merely what he sought, his name would not have had so large a place in our history. To be known as Hernando de Soto, the first white man to behold the Mississippi River, is a distinction not to be equaled by the finding of untold wealth.

Not realizing what the discovery meant, De Soto was still bent on continuing his search for gold. Perhaps it lay just across this great river. At any rate he would find out. Soon all hands were busy building rafts to carry the little army to the other side.

Spanish Soldiers Making Their Way
through the Forests of the New World

There the weary search began again. For many months De Soto wandered over the country on the west bank of the Mississippi. Still no gold. With the disappointment and the hardships he was fast wearing out. Then he caught a fever and soon died.

The condition of his followers was pitiful. Between their sorrow at the loss of their leader and their fear of the Indians, they did not know where to turn.

You see De Soto had told the Indians that he was a Child of the Sun, and that death could not touch him. So they had a wholesome fear of him. What if they should find out now that De Soto was dead! Nothing was more likely than that they would at once attack and kill his men. In some way his death must be kept secret.

So, prompted by fear and moving like ghosts, the men wrapped their leader in a cloak, weighted it down with sand, and at midnight silently lowered him into the quiet waters of the Mississippi River. Then, telling the Indians that he had gone to heaven for a short visit and would soon be back, they broke camp and started for home on foot. Later they made boats and floated down the Mississippi River to the Gulf of Mexico.

Of the gay six hundred who sailed away from Cuba in 1539, only three hundred, half-starved and wretched, reached the Spanish settlements in Mexico to tell the story of De Soto's great discovery.

VI

SIR FRANCIS DRAKE

Drake and Sir John Hawkins

FOR the first half of the sixteenth century Spain practically ruled the seas. Her ships came and went across the Atlantic, and her trade was the greatest of any European nation's.

About the middle of this same century Elizabeth became queen of England; and during her reign, England, too, grew to be a great maritime power. Spain soon came to look upon England as a rival, and these two nations kept close watch of each other's every move.

In 1562 three English vessels sailed down the western coast of Africa. They were headed for Guinea, to carry out what seemed to be a fine scheme on the part of their commander, John Hawkins.

Hawkins's plan was to go to Guinea, load his ship with negroes, carry them to the West Indies, and sell them as slaves. And this is just what he did. Three hundred black men were crowded into his three ships and taken to the island of Haiti. Here these negroes and certain English goods that Hawkins had brought along were traded for sugar, hides, pearls, and spices. And so large was Hawkins's profit that, by the time his last slave was sold, he was forced to charter two extra vessels to carry away all his wealth.

At that time it was not considered wrong to deal in slaves, and John Hawkins's successful trip brought him great honor in England. But Philip II, the Spanish king, did not want, and would not have, Englishmen trading with the West Indies. The strictest orders were at once sent to the islands that no goods whatever were to be bought from the English.

An English Ship of Private Ownership, about the Time of Sir John Hawkins

Nothing daunted, however, John Hawkins soon repeated his voyage; and this time his profits were even greater than on the first trip. If the authorities of any port refused to trade with him, he merely landed one hundred men in armor and frightened the Spaniards into doing as he wished. His fame was greater than ever in England, and on his return Queen Elizabeth knighted him.

Now Sir John Hawkins had a young cousin in England named Francis Drake. As a boy Drake had been apprenticed to the owner of a channel coaster. It was hard service, and the boy had a bad time. Still he did his duty so well and seemed so at home on the sea that he completely won the old skipper's heart. When the old man died, he left his ship to Drake.

It was very natural, however, that, hearing of John Hawkins's wonderful success, young Drake should not be content with a mere channel coaster. So he sold his vessel; and when his famous cousin started on a third voyage, Francis Drake commanded one of his ships. This was in 1567, the year Drake was twenty-two years old.

First of all they went to Africa where they loaded their ships with negroes, and then the expedition sailed as before for the West Indies. And, as before, a market for the slaves was found, though, because of King Philip's orders, much of the trading had to be done secretly by night.

Finally the time to think of starting for home arrived. But at least two of the ships had stood the voyage so badly that they had to be repaired before they could be trusted on the open sea. For this purpose the little fleet boldly entered the Spanish port of San Juan de Ulua.

Here, riding peacefully at anchor, they were surprised by the approach of a Spanish fleet. The English ships certainly had the advantage, as they lay snugly in the port, and the Spanish vessels could not enter without the risk of being sunk by the English guns.

The commanders of the two fleets held a conference, and Hawkins agreed to let the Spanish ships enter the port on condition that the English should be allowed to repair their vessels before putting out to sea. All this was readily agreed to, and the Spaniards sailed into the port.

You would think that by this time Hawkins would have known the crafty Spanish nature too well to take such a risk. Before many days had passed, the Spaniards had turned on the English, and a fierce fight had taken place. When it was over only two ships of Hawkins's fleet were left. And these two—one under the command of Hawkins, and the other in charge of young Francis Drake—had a weary time getting back to England.

Drake the Voyager and Fighter—Magellan

FRANCIS DRAKE's experience at San Juan de Ulua would have been quite enough to discourage the average man. He had lost money and friends by that piece of Spanish treachery, and he and his men had endured many trials on the voyage home.

But far from being disheartened, Drake was soon ready to sail again for the Spanish ports in America. He had two objects in mind when he started from England: on his own account, he meant to seize treasures enough from the Spaniards to repay himself for his losses at their hands; and he hoped to aid his Queen at home by crippling her rival's American colonies.

Judging by the results, Drake must have felt well

satisfied. He made three such voyages on which he raided Spanish ships, took Spanish prisoners, and made himself a veritable terror to the Spanish settlements in the West Indies and along the Gulf of Mexico.

On his third voyage, Drake and his men landed on the Isthmus of Panama. Afoot they started inland to waylay a cargo of treasures which they knew was being brought across the Isthmus. In some way the Spaniards were warned and eluded Drake. Yet great results were to come from his effort to meet them.

Sir Francis Drake

Working their way through the dark, dense forests where no sunlight ever came, Drake and his men finally reached a mountain peak. And climbing a great tree Drake looked out over the forests and saw, stretching north, south, and west, the shining blue waves of the Pacific Ocean. He seems to have been as deeply stirred by the sight as Balboa was sixty years before.

From his seat high up in the tree, Drake thanked God that he had been permitted to be the first Englishman

Magellan Planting the Cross in the Philippine Islands

to see this mighty ocean, and prayed that he might "sail once in an English ship on that sea."

This was on February 11, 1573. On the 9th of August, Drake and his men reached the shores of Plymouth, England.

Then for a while Drake stayed at home. But he could not forget his wish to take an English ship into the Pacific Ocean. Moreover, he wanted some of the wealth of Peru and Mexico; and he did not believe it wrong to take from the Spaniards what they had seized from the natives.

Years before, in fact during the very time Cortez was busy conquering Mexico, an adventurous navigator, a Portugese sailing under the Spanish flag, had made a wonderful voyage. This bold sailor was Ferdinand Magellan. Down the eastern coast of South America he had slowly made his way until he had reached the straits which now bear his name. Then, passing through the straits, he had entered the Pacific, had crossed that great ocean, and had discovered the Philippine Islands. Here Magellan was killed by the natives; but his sailors, going on, had reached Spain in 1522, having sailed entirely around the globe.

Francis Drake now planned to reach Peru by following Magellan's course and sailing around South America. In November, 1577, he embarked from Plymouth with five ships and one hundred and sixty-four men. For fifty-four days they saw no land. Then the shores of Brazil came in sight. At last the Straits of Magellan were reached and Drake passed through them.

His flagship, the *Golden Hind,* was the only one of his fleet that entered the Pacific. The other ships either had turned back or had come to grief on the rocks.

Ferdinand Magellan

To attack the Spanish ports of Peru with one ship certainly seemed foolhardy. But Drake perhaps realized that these ports had no real defense. You see the Spaniards themselves carried their cargoes across the Isthmus of Panama, because a southern route was considered very dangerous and very long. And without doubt it never entered a Spanish mind that any foe would come that way, or that defense was needed. So, sailing bravely up the coast of Chili, Francis Drake, in his single ship advanced on Peru.

It seemed almost as if the Spanish gold, silver, and jewels must have been just waiting to be seized. Into port after port the *Golden Hind* dashed and came out again richer by enormous sums. Ship after ship fell an easy prey to her English captain. Surprise was on every hand, resistance nowhere.

At last, with plunder valued at millions of dollars, Drake was satisfied. Now he turned his attention to searching for some new passage by water from the Pacific to the Atlantic. Carefully examining the shores, he sailed north along the coast of California as far as the bay of San Francisco.

Here he gave up his search and resolved to go home by way of the Pacific. According to custom, however, before starting he took possession for Queen Elizabeth of the land he had been exploring, and called it New Albion.

After crossing the Pacific Ocean Drake rounded the Cape of Good Hope and sailed once more into the Plymouth port, in September, 1580.

Queen Elizabeth hesitated at first about recognizing this bold subject who had plundered so many Spanish settlements. She was afraid of angering still further the Spanish king. But she decided in Drake's favor, and consented to pay him a visit on the *Golden Hind*. As was only fitting, Drake had a splendid banquet served in her honor. Then Elizabeth asked Drake to kneel before her, and in the presence of his many guests she knighted the brave mariner, who had first carried the English flag around the world.

On Board the "Golden Hind":
Queen Elizabeth Knighting Francis Drake

Elizabeth also gave orders that the *Golden Hind* should be preserved, but after a hundred years it fell to pieces. Out of the timbers a chair was made, which may still be seen at Oxford. So ended Sir Francis Drake's ship.

Drake had already risked and accomplished more than most men do in a lifetime, but his services were still to be demanded in other ways. At one time he was appointed Mayor of Plymouth, and later he served on a royal commission to inquire into the state of the Navy. Associated with him on this commission was Sir Walter Raleigh, of whom you shall hear more. And to the friendship of this knight Drake came to owe much.

In 1585 war was declared between England and

Spain. Once more Drake crossed the Atlantic and wrought dreadful havoc among the Spanish colonies in America; and, when he got back to England, a still more dangerous undertaking was asked of him.

Philip II of Spain was collecting a great battle fleet, or armada, for the invasion of England. Queen Elizabeth sent Drake with thirty ships to destroy the enemy's storehouses and powder magazines. He entered the harbor of Cadiz early one morning and before many hours had burned upward of ten thousand tons of shipping, a feat which he afterwards called "singeing the beard of the King of Spain." It took Philip a whole year to repair the damages that Drake had done, and this gave England time to prepare for war.

An English Battleship of Elizabeth's Reign

When the Spanish Armada came in 1588 to invade England, Drake was appointed vice admiral under Lord Howard and served under him in the fighting that resulted in the destruction of the Armada.

Several years later, Sir Francis Drake and Sir John Hawkins were again trying to crush the power of Spain in America. But the old success was not with them. They were repulsed by the Spaniards, sickness broke out, and Sir John Hawkins died off the coast of Porto Rico.

This death, the sickness of his men, and the apparent failure of his voyage were all keenly felt by Drake. For some time he struggled to succeed in spite of the great odds against him. But at last he, too, fell ill and in a few days died. His men buried him at sea, and thus ended the life of one of England's bravest and boldest navigators.

VII

SIR WALTER RALEIGH

Sir Walter Raleigh and Sir Humphrey Gilbert

SIR WALTER RALEIGH was a brave and gallant English knight who lived during the reign of Queen Elizabeth. The story is told that one day, as the Queen approached the place where he was waiting with a crowd to see her pass, she paused before a muddy spot in the way. Raleigh, without a moment's hesitation, slipped his velvet cape from his shoulders and spread it out for her to walk on. This little act of courtesy greatly pleased Queen Elizabeth, and ever after she remembered her gallant knight.

Raleigh was born in a seaport town of Devonshire in 1552. Here large sailing vessels used to anchor to load and unload their cargoes.

When a boy, Raleigh was like all other boys. There was nothing he enjoyed quite so much as going down to the wharves and hearing the sailors tell thrilling stories of the sea and the strange countries they had visited. Then Raleigh would say to himself, "When I am a man, I, too, will discover some new land." And though he never discovered a new land, he did much in attempting to found an English colony in America.

Since the Cabots crossed the Atlantic, England had not sent out many exploring expeditions. But, as you know, Spain had done so; and her colonies were growing stronger than those of any other European nation, and her trade was greater.

Sir Walter Raleigh

Never the best of friends with Spain, England naturally did not like to see Spain gaining more power than she herself across the sea. So, not to be outdone, the English made plans for planting colonies in America and for carrying on a larger trade with that country.

Moreover, England had other reasons for wanting to colonize America besides the desire to increase her trade and to hold her own with Spain. There was always the old hope of finding gold; and there was yet a fourth reason, one that had grown out of the condition of the English people themselves.

In the time of Queen Elizabeth, the population of England was about five millions, and there was not work enough in the kingdom to keep so many people employed. Hundreds could find nothing to do. So, while the rich in England were growing richer each day, the poor were growing poorer.

Why not send these poor idle people to America? There they would certainly have plenty of work and a fair chance to make a new start in life.

Colonists Waiting to Board Ship for Virginia

Of course this would mean a great risk and vast sums of money, and there were few persons who cared to hazard all they owned in an undertaking that might be unsuccessful. Again, how many people do you suppose would willingly be separated forever from their friends in England?

Yet, in spite of the risk, there were some wealthy men in England who put great sums of money into ships to carry colonists across the ocean. One of these was Sir Humphrey Gilbert, a stepbrother of Walter Raleigh. In 1578 he set sail with seven ships to plant a colony in North America. His first attempt was unsuccessful.

On his second voyage Sir Humphrey landed in Newfoundland and claimed it in the name of the Queen. From there he sailed south to the Kennebec River. As his three vessels skirted the coast, a great storm arose. Suddenly with a crash the largest ship crushed its bows against a hidden rock and sank.

The storm continued to rage wildly. Sir Humphrey decided to head for England. Soon his little ship began to founder in the terrible sea. Sitting near the stern the brave man called out to his companions on the other vessel, "The way to heaven is as near by sea as by land." That night his ship went down, and neither he nor his sailors were ever seen again.

Sir Walter Raleigh and His Colony

ON the death of Sir Humphrey Gilbert, Walter Raleigh decided to carry out his stepbrother's scheme. He was a rich man and a great favorite with the Queen. He asked her to renew in his name the charter granted to Sir Humphrey, and the Queen gladly did so.

These charters gave in writing the privileges the Queen was willing to grant her colonists. It was so far from England to America, and the journey back and forth took so long, that it would have been impossible to refer questions to the Queen as they came up. The only way was to decide ahead what the colonists should be allowed to do. Then if the people who were to sail to the new land felt that they could be content under those conditions, all well and good. Otherwise they had better stay in England.

Walter Raleigh's charter granted him the right to explore and settle the eastern coast of America and to make himself governor of any colony he might found. The colonists who went with him were to have all the political and religious rights and privileges that they had in England.

This was a very fair charter. Everything seemed to promise success to the future colonists. But to make assurance doubly sure, Raleigh thought best to send an exploring party ahead, so that when the colonists reached America they would know what to expect. With this in view, two vessels sailed away from England in 1584.

Their anchors were cast just off the island of Roanoke; and going ashore the English found the climate delightful, the vegetation rich, and the Indians most eager to welcome them. For several weeks the explorers stayed on the island; and such a good time did they have that, when they got back to England, they gave only glowing reports of all they had seen. Queen Elizabeth was so delighted when she heard of the glorious regions across the sea, that she named them Virginia, in her own honor. Elizabeth was not married and was proud of her title, "The Virgin Queen." As a reward for his efforts in the new land, Raleigh was knighted and became Sir

Walter Raleigh.

Now there was nothing to delay the sending out of the colony, and soon the well-laden ships were on their way. In time Roanoke was reached, and the men and their goods were put safely ashore.

Queen Elizabeth

So far so good. But from this time matters did not progress. The colonists were lazy. Instead of exerting themselves in tilling the ground and building homes, they wasted their time and lived on what they could get from the Indians. Of course the Indians did not like this arrangement. The English were only a burden to them, and constant quarrels arose.

The next year Sir Francis Drake sailed up to Virginia to see how the colonists were getting along. He found them almost destitute and terribly homesick; and, yielding to their pleadings, he carried them back to England.

As far as founding a colony was concerned, the expedition had proved a failure. However, it brought about two results which became of great value to England. On their return Sir Walter's colonists presented him with two kinds of plants which they had found growing on Roanoke Island. One was the potato, which, up to this time, the English had never known. They tried it and liked it so well that it has ever since been raised in their land.

The other plant was tobacco, which the colonists had tried and had deemed worthy of being carried all the way to England.

Pipes Which the Colonists Found in Use by the Indians

Sir Walter tried the tobacco; and he, too, liked it. An amusing tale is told of what happened to Sir Walter one day as he was smoking. His servant, who had never before seen smoke come out of anyone's mouth, came into the room. He glanced at his master, thought he must be on fire, and rushed out for a jug of water, which he promptly poured all over Sir Walter to put out the fire.

In 1587 Sir Walter Raleigh made another effort to colonize America. This time the colonists included women and children as well as men.

Soon after they landed on Roanoke a little girl was born. She was the first child of English parents to be born in America. Her name was Virginia Dare, and she was the granddaughter of John White, the deputy governor of the colony.

Before long Deputy Governor White sailed back to England for new supplies. When he started, the colonists told him that, if for any reason they left Roanoke Island, they would carve on a tree the name of the place where he could find them; and that, if they were in any trouble when they moved, he would see a cross cut above the name.

Three years passed before Governor White came back to the island, and by that time there was no one to receive him. He could not find a single one of the colonists. Their homes were deserted, and the harbor was empty. Not a trace was left excepting the word "Croatoan" cut into the trunk of a tree, but there was no cross over the name. Croatoan was the name of an island not far away. But though search after search was made, not one of the missing colonists was ever found on that island or anywhere else.

Saddened and disappointed by the fate of his colonists, Sir Walter Raleigh gave up his idea of personally founding an English settlement in America. His experiment had cost him over forty thousand pounds. However, he still held firmly to his belief that this country would one day be an English nation.

Stimulated by his example, others followed his lead with happier results. After a few years, more and more English people crossed to America, and many English colonies were established along the eastern coast.

On this site, in July-August, 1585 (O.S.), colonists, sent out from England by Sir Walter Raleigh, built a fort, called by them "The New Fort in Virginia." These colonists were the first settlers of the English race in America. They returned to England in July, 1586, with Sir Francis Drake. Near this place was born, on the 18th of August, 1587, Virginia Dare, the first child of English Parents born in America–daughter of Ananias Dare and Eleanor White, his wife, members of another band of colonists sent out by Sir Walter Raleigh in 1587. On Sunday, August 20, 1587, Virginia Dare was baptized. Manteo, the friendly Chief of the Hatteras Indians had been baptized on the Sunday preceding. These baptisms are the first known celebrations of a Christian Sacrament in the territory of the thirteen original United States.

The colonists soon realized that they had to work in order to live. They built comfortable homes, raised crops, and traded among themselves. They laid the foundations of such towns as Jamestown and Plymouth, which in the course of time became centers of trade with the mother country. In fact the English colonists who followed Sir Walter Raleigh's example succeeded by their hard and earnest work in turning a wilderness into the prosperous land of an English-speaking nation.

VIII

JOHN SMITH AND POCAHONTAS

The Jamestown Colony and the Adventures of John Smith

IN the year 1606 two companies were formed in England to make settlements in America. One of these was called the London Company, the other the Plymouth Company.

On the first day of January, 1607, the London Company sent out three vessels with one hundred and five colonists, all men. Of these, fifty-two were men of wealthy families who had never had to work. This was very unfortunate for a colony that had to make its way in an unfarmed land.

The colonists had been told to put ashore on Roanoke Island, where Raleigh's ill-fated colonists had been. But a storm drove the ships into Chesapeake Bay, and the newcomers sailed up a beautiful river which they named after King James. It was now the middle of May. The place looked inviting; the shores were covered with beautiful flowers and shrubs, and so the colonists determined to settle there. They built a little town and named it Jamestown.

But it was not an easy task—this founding a colony. The food gave out. The hot Virginia sun and the terrible fever killed many. Within a few months half of the settlers had died, and the remainder would have starved had not some kind Indians brought corn and fruit.

In time, however, the intense heat of summer gave

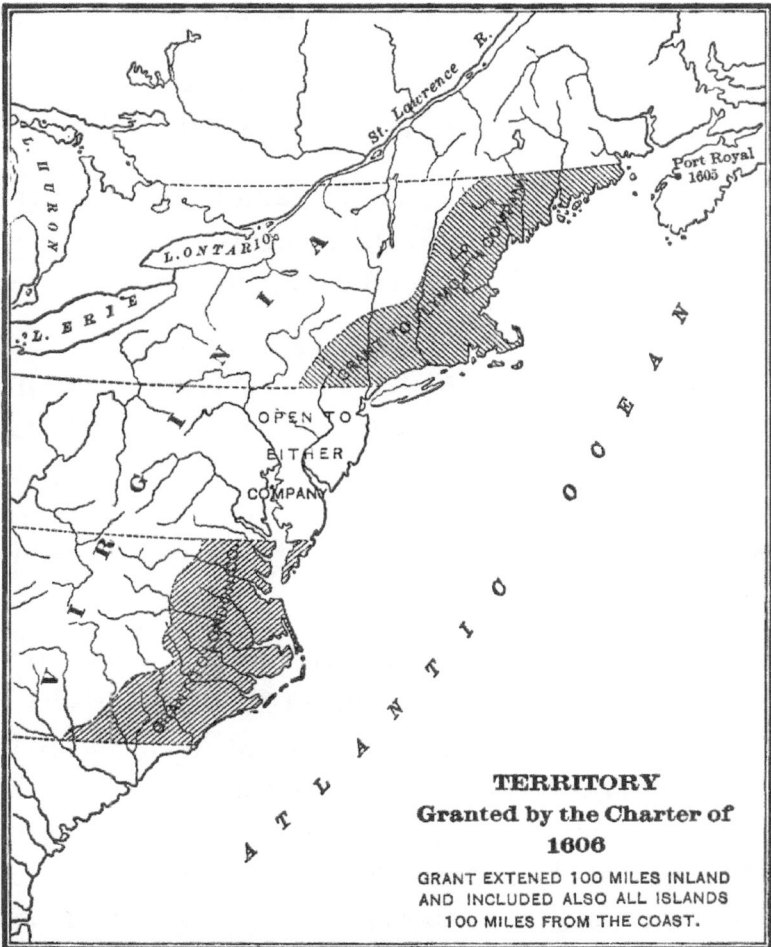

TERRITORY
Granted by the Charter of
1606

GRANT EXTENDED 100 MILES INLAND
AND INCLUDED ALSO ALL ISLANDS
100 MILES FROM THE COAST.

place to the glorious days of autumn, and the settlers became hopeful again.

By great good fortune there was a wonderful man in this colony, and had it not been for him the settlers at Jamestown might all have perished. This was Captain John Smith. Through his ability and good judgment, the colony finally won its footing.

John Smith was born in 1579, in England. His life was one of continuous adventure, much of which he tells in his

James I of England

autobiography. Many think that he has exaggerated his accounts of his daring adventures and narrow escapes from death; but he was nevertheless a wonderful man, and his life as he tells it is very interesting.

When yet a boy Smith was very fond of adventure. He was anxious to travel and see strange lands, so at the age of fifteen he sold his books and ran away with the money. He went over to the continent of Europe and fought in the Dutch and French armies.

He soon tired of this and thought he would like to go on a ship; so he boarded a vessel sailing to Italy. A severe storm arose; and the sailors, thinking him the cause of the tempest, threw him, like Jonah, into the sea. But young Smith was a fine swimmer and after a

hard struggle reached an island.

A passing vessel picked him up. This ship was a war vessel. It soon met an enemy, and a battle ensued. Smith fought so bravely that he was given a share in the plunder of the vessel.

From the original engraving in John Smith's "Historie of New England, Virginia, and The Summer Isles," published in 1624.

Still looking for other adventures, our young hero turned his steps toward the east, where he joined the Austrian army, which was fighting the Turks. For his bravery he was made a captain.

One day the Turks sent a challenge "to any officer in the Christian army" that "to delight the ladies who did long to see any courtlike pastime, the Lord Turbashaw did defy any captain that had the command of a company, who durst combat him for his head." This challenge was accepted by so many young captains that they had to cast lots, and the lot fell to Captain John Smith.

All the officers and soldiers and grand ladies appeared to witness the conflict. With one single swift thrust Smith sent his lance through his opponent. A comrade of the Turk wanted to avenge his friend's death. He challenged Smith, but a like fate awaited him. Still a third Turk thought he could overcome Smith, but he too was killed. For his skill Smith was given a coat of arms on which the bleeding heads of three Turks were represented.

Ill luck soon overtook him, however. He was wounded in a battle and left on the battlefield as dead. Lying there with dead and dying men on all sides, he was finally found and his wounds cared for. After a while, Smith was taken to Constantinople and sold as a slave. A Turkish lady aided him, but he was cruelly treated by her brother.

One day while Smith was threshing grain, this cruel master rode up and insulted him. In his anger he smote the man and killed him. Then he swiftly exchanged his ragged clothes for those of his master and, hiding the body under some straw, fled.

After traveling through other countries our adventurer arrived in England, just as the fever of American colonization was at its height. And he, too, determined to go to America.

Life in Jamestown

In 1607 Captain John Smith sailed with a colonizing expedition sent out by the London company. It was the same expedition that founded Jamestown, as we have seen, and struggled through that first hot summer.

Many of the colonists, you will remember, had

never worked. They thought manual labor a disgrace. But it soon became evident that some must work, or all would starve. The warm climate had tended to make them all languid. Many were really lazy and preferred to search for gold than till the soil.

But John Smith soon showed these idle "gentlemen" how to hew trees and build huts. In his book he says, "The axes so oft blistered their tender fingers, that many times every third blow had a loud oath to drown the echo." Smith did not like to hear the men swear, so he devised a plan to make them refrain from it. He told them that at night, for every oath, he would pour a can of cold water down the swearer's sleeve.

At first it was very hard to get food enough. The corn brought by the friendly Indians did not last long. So to keep the colonists from starving, Smith explored the country, visited different Indian tribes, and bargained with them for such supplies as they could furnish.

These settlers had no idea of the greatness of this country. A map of that time showed Virginia as a mere narrow strip of land between the Atlantic and the Pacific. Believing this to be true, Captain Smith decided to visit the Pacific and went on many exploring trips to the west of Jamestown in the hope of finding it.

On one of these expeditions, Captain Smith and a few of his men fell into the hands of hostile Indians. All of his companions were killed, but Smith was saved by his presence of mind. He diverted the Indians' attention by showing them a compass. The Indians had never seen anything like it before. They thought it marvelous.

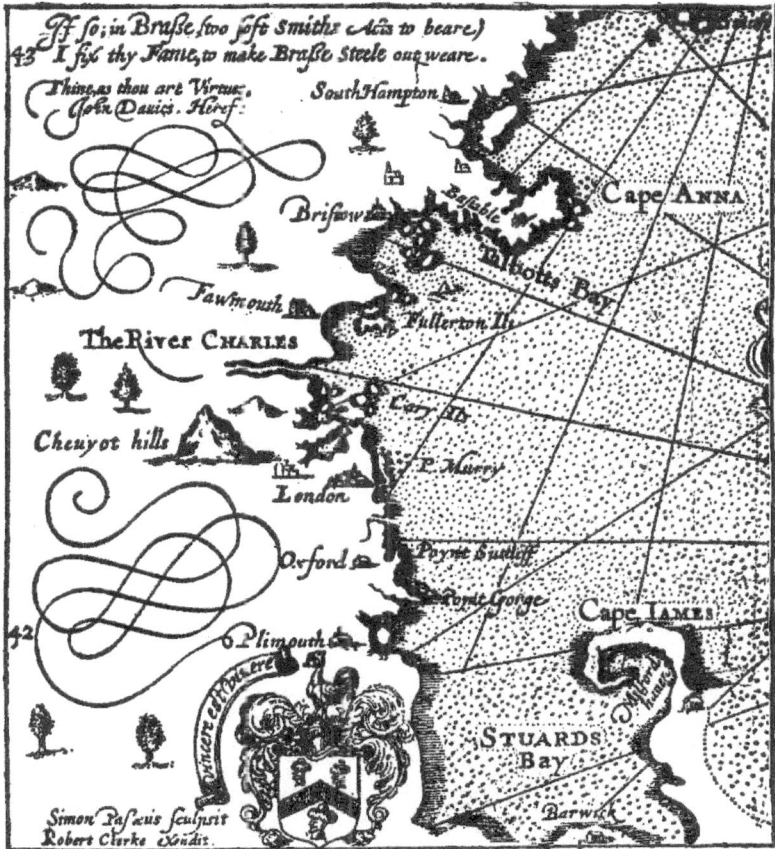

*Part of John Smith's Map of New England,
from Smith's "Historie" of 1624*

Then Smith wrote some message on a piece of paper and asked his captors to send it to Jamestown. When the Indians found that this wonderful prisoner "could make paper talk" to his friends, they were a little afraid of him and considered it wiser not to kill him, but to take him to their mighty chief, Powhatan.

When John Smith was led as a captive before Powhatan, the great chief sat before his fire, dressed in raccoon skins. On either side of him sat the squaws, and in front of the squaws stood the grim warriors, straight and stiff. It was a terrible moment for poor Captain Smith. Would they kill him at once, or could he still hope to save his life by amusing the Indians? Again the compass was brought out, and once more it worked a charm. The chief concluded to keep this entertaining person a prisoner.

Now, Powhatan had a little daughter twelve or thirteen years old. Her name was Pocahontas. She was a beautiful girl and her father's pet. She was allowed to spend much time with the old chief's prisoner; and Smith told her strange stories, made whistles for her, gave her strings of beads, and so won her lasting love and affection.

But before very long the novelty of the prisoner's compass and the marvel of his writing wore away. Smith had nothing new with which to amuse the Indians. They grew tired of him, and Powhatan ordered him to be killed. The day of the execution arrived. The whole tribe came. Smith was forced to lay his head on a block of stone. An Indian had just raised the hatchet for the fatal blow when Pocahontas rushed to Smith and, throwing her arms over his head, begged her father to spare his life. The old chief could never refuse his little daughter anything; and so Smith's life was spared, and he was sent back to Jamestown.

From now on Pocahontas was always kind to the colonists; and as long as there was peace between the Indians and the English, she often visited them. Once

C: Smith takes the King of Pafpahegh prisoner A.º 1609.

From the drawing in Smith's "Historie" of 1624

she even came secretly by night and warned them of danger from an Indian attack.

When Captain Smith reached the colony again, he found it in a sad condition. During his imprisonment, matters had gone from bad to worse. With him away the lazy would not work, and nothing seemed to have been done. Sickness and famine had once more attacked the settlers, and death was everywhere. Fortunately a vessel with provisions and more colonists soon anchored in the bay. But many of the newcomers were "fine gentlemen" or "vagabond gentlemen" like the first settlers. They too refused to do their share. "We have not come here to work," they boldly asserted. "If you will not work, you shall not eat," said Smith; and they soon found that he fully meant what he said. They had to work, and matters began to improve. Still the temptation to neglect the fields and to search for gold was very strong with these early settlers. Once they found something that looked like gold. A shipload was sent to England. Great was the disappointment when they learned it was nothing but yellow earth. It was called "fool's gold."

In the fall of 1609 Smith was dreadfully injured by the explosion of a bag of gunpowder, and he was compelled to go to England for surgical aid.

But as before, no sooner was he gone than the troubles of the colonists began to increase. Now came what was known as the "starving time." At last the colonists had to eat cats, dogs, rats; and, once, even an Indian was cooked and devoured. If more help had not come from England just when it did, the little colony would soon have been at an end.

However, it was not until Sir Thomas Dale came to Virginia as governor that affairs really began to brighten. A stern, severe soldier, Governor Dale had strict rules and saw that they were obeyed. If a colonist did not like the rules and talked against them, the Governor had a hole bored through his tongue; and he had other punishments for other offenses. So it is no wonder that from the time of his coming the harvests were greater and the idlers disappeared.

But in spite of all Governor Dale could do, one great danger still threatened the colonists. This was the hostility of the Indians. They were very treacherous. Even Powhatan had played several wily tricks upon the white settlers and had proved a most dangerous friend.

Such were the conditions between the white men and the Indians, when, by chance, a certain young colonial captain captured Pocahontas. She was visiting a neighboring tribe; and with a copper kettle he bribed the chief of this tribe to help him take the Indian girl prisoner. Then he carried her back to Jamestown where she was kept as a hostage for her father's good behavior.

Portrait of Pocahontas Made in England in 1616

In the years that had passed since Pocahontas saved the life of John Smith, she had grown still more beautiful. Living among the settlers, she quickly came to be beloved by all, and especially by a young Englishman named John Rolfe. He wanted to make her his wife. But she was still a heathen, and it was thought wrong to marry a heathen. So Pocahontas became a Christian, was baptized in the little church at Jamestown, and received the name of Rebecca. And the next year, 1614, she and John Rolfe were married. Both the settlers and the Indians were delighted over this marriage, for it created a strong, new bond between them. Many years of peace followed.

Later Rolfe took his bride to England where the King and Queen received this American princess with great delight, for they had heard of her bravery in saving Captain Smith's life.

In 1617, John Rolfe decided to return with his wife and their little son to Jamestown. Pocahontas had grown to love her adopted country, and yet she had many sad hours of longing for her forest home. But this home she was never to see again. Just before she and her husband were to sail, she suddenly became ill and died. And the beautiful Indian princess was buried in the land of her adoption, where her sweet winning manners had won her many friends.

Two years before his marriage to Pocahontas, John Rolfe had begun the systematic culture of tobacco in Virginia. Soon this came to be the leading industry of the colony.

In 1619 a Dutch vessel sold twenty negroes to the settlers. They were made to till the soil and do manual labor. From time to time more slaves were brought over, and slavery and the culture of tobacco went hand in hand.

Tobacco was becoming very popular in England and found a ready sale, though King James was much opposed to the smoking of it. He called it "a vile weed." As it continued to be smoked just the same, he placed a heavy tax upon it. Yet, in spite of even this, the demand increased; and a flourishing tobacco trade with Europe resulted in a flourishing colony in America.

What had become of Captain John Smith? After his gunpowder wounds had healed, he had come back to America and explored the Atlantic coast from Maine many miles to the south. It was he who gave to this part of our country the name New England. He carefully made a map of the new section and on his return to England presented it to King Charles, the son of King James.

Then the next year Smith set out again to found a colony in this region. Unfortunately he and his vessel were captured by the French, but after a while Smith escaped and fled back to England. He never returned to America after this, but remained in England and wrote several books on his travels.

John Smith has been called "The Father of Virginia." Certain it is that it was through his bravery, tact, and resolute perseverance that the Jamestown colony weathered its first hard year in America and became one of the most important English settlements in the New World.

The Indians

THE Virginia colonists, the explorers who came to America before them, and the settlers who followed them, all found the country occupied by Indians.

These Indians had copper-colored skins, were tall, and had small black piercing eyes and straight black hair.

The race was divided into tribes, and each tribe was governed by its chief. Each tribe had its headquarters in some definite part of the country, although the men in hunting often wandered for miles into neighboring lands.

The homes of the Indians varied according to the tribe. Some lived in log houses, some built rude houses of bark, while still other tribes had only circular wigwams. There was no chimney in any of these homes. The fires were built in fire pits dug in the ground, and the smoke escaped through a hole in the roof.

The most important of the Indians' household goods was the pot. They had also some wooden dishes and trays, which they made themselves. They seldom had anything to sit upon, but squatted upon the ground. Some of them slept on small couches made of bulrushes. Others rolled themselves in skins and slept on the ground.

The Indian's clothes were generally made from the dried skins of animals. He would wear the same skin until it wore out, and never thought of washing it. Cleanliness was little known among these people. They were very fond of bright colors and liked to deck themselves with strings of shells or beads. In this love of finery, the men exceeded the women.

The Indians lived mainly on game and fish. The game consisted of wild geese, ducks, deer, bears, and foxes. In summer, game was very plentiful and easily found; but a struggle for existence began with the cold weather.

Indians Making a Canoe from the Trunk of a Tree

The Indian despised manual labor. He spent his time in fishing, hunting, and fighting, and left all the hard work to his squaw. These squaws must have had their hands full, as they had to look after the house, the planting of the garden, the children, and the cooking.

An Indian mother was anxious to have each son grow up to be a manly, brave warrior. His first lesson was not to read and write, but to use his bow and arrow. The little girls learned such housework as the Indians thought necessary and helped their mothers in the garden.

Among some of the Indian tribes the women held a high place and were often consulted in matters of war and peace. Most of the Indian women were kind and gentle, but the men were usually very cruel.

An Indian warrior's bravery was judged by the number of human scalps that hung from his belt. This prize trophy was cut from the head of each victim, sometimes even before he was dead. Because of this custom of cutting off scalps, the Indian warriors adopted a strange way of wearing their hair.

Indian Stone Ax

Most likely it was partly to show that they did not fear death and partly as a challenge to their enemies to come and take their scalps if they could. Be that as it may, an Indian warrior had his hair cut short except on the top of his head. Here grew one long lock— the scalp lock.

If an enemy was taken alive, he could be pretty sure that sooner or later he must die by torture. His only hope was that some member of his captor's tribe might ask that his life be spared. If this miracle should happen, the prisoner would be adopted as a

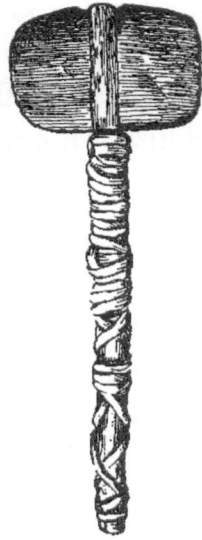

Indian War Club

member of the victorious tribe.

A favorite method of putting a prisoner to death was by burning him alive. He was tied to a stump, and fagots were piled around him and set on fire. The delight of the Indians at this awful sight was often so great that they would dance and howl like fiends around the poor victim.

The war implements of the Indians were tomahawks, bows and arrows, and war clubs. The tomahawk looked much like a hatchet, but was made of stone. Later when the Indian saw the white man's weapons, he wanted to obtain them. For a long time gunpowder was a mystery to the savages. They thought that it grew from the ground. One of the Indian tribes sowed some in the spring, hoping that by autumn they would have a fine harvest.

In warfare an Indian seldom came out in open battle, but preferred to send a swift arrow upon an unsuspecting foe. If he could kill his enemy, why should he endanger himself? so he reasoned.

The religious beliefs of the Indian were simple. The Great Spirit, all wise, loving, and powerful, ruled over all. But the spirit of some animal ruled and took care of each individual. An Indian never killed the animal whose spirit formed his *totem*, but he did not hesitate to kill the totem of any other Indian. After death, the spirits of the brave would go to the happy hunting grounds, where hunting and fishing and eating were the chief pastimes.

The Indians did not have a priesthood. The

medicine-man had some of the qualities of a priest. He pretended to be able to drive away evil spirits by the aid of magic.

The Indian's education was a very severe one. He knew nothing about reading and writing, although he did make pictures which served as a kind of writing. But he was skilled in woodcraft, in the art of war, and, above all, in self-control.

It would not be at all fair to say that the American Indian was always cruel and revengeful. He had a good side to his nature which was just as strong as the bad side. No friend could prove truer than an Indian. He never forgot a kindness that had been done to him, and never failed to return it in some way. He would often divide his last ear of corn with a starving person. It was only after the settlers had shown hostility to the Indians that they found them the bitterest and most persistent of foes.

Calumet, or Indian Peace Pipe

IX

MILES STANDISH AND THE PILGRIMS

Why the Pilgrims Left England

THREE hundred years ago the kings of England had almost absolute power. The people had very few rights, either in church or government.

When James I came to the English throne he held the same views as the rulers before him. He said, "I am the King and therefore can do no wrong." He said also that everybody must attend his church and worship in just the way he did.

Now, there were a great many good people in England at this time who did not agree with the King's religious views. Neither the king nor the bishop should be the head of the church, they argued. They thought that the churches were built too grandly for a house of God and that too much stress was laid upon the outward forms of religion.

Having these views, it was impossible for them to conform to the rules of the Established Church. So they separated from the Church of England and held services according to their own ideas in their own churches and in private homes. In consequence they were called Separatists.

King James became greatly indignant with the Separatists and finally made a law forcing everybody to attend his church and no other.

The Separatists, however, firm in their own belief, said that they would not and could not obey this law. Instead of giving up their religion, they loved it still more and resolved to suffer and, if need be, die for it. Yet they were cautious. They no longer held public meetings, but gathered together privately to worship God. Oftentimes numbers of them journeyed from place to place, that they might carry on their services unmolested; and for this reason these wanderers became known as Pilgrims as well as Separatists. Still, in spite of all their precautions, the King's watchful officials, whenever possible, would imprison them, fine them heavily, and often lead them to the gallows.

At last, in 1608, a company of Pilgrims from the town of Scrooby decided to flee to Holland, where religious freedom was granted to all. But just as they were about to embark, the King's officers rushed up and seized them. Their clothes were taken away, and they were thrust into prison, where they were kept for several months.

The following year these Pilgrims again decided to leave England. This time they arrived safely in Holland. At last they had perfect religious freedom. They no longer lived in fear of spying officials or dark prisons.

From time to time other bands of Pilgrims came from England, until in a few years several hundreds of English were living on Dutch soil. They lived there very happily for almost twelve years. The Dutch liked them because they were good and diligent citizens, and they in turn liked the thrifty Dutch.

But as the years passed, these Pilgrims were not so well satisfied as at first. They saw that their children were acquiring the Dutch language, Dutch ways and customs, and were forgetting all about England. It must be remembered that although the Pilgrims wanted religious liberty, they dearly loved England and always had been true English at heart. It hurt them to see their children gradually becoming Dutch. Then, too, they thought, the Dutch were not so religious as themselves and were setting their children a bad example.

Owing to all this, the Pilgrims at length decided to seek another country. They thought of several places, but none seemed so desirable as America. Surely here, if anywhere, they could found a little colony of their own and live unmolested the life that pleased them best.

The Pilgrims in America

THERE were about a thousand Pilgrims in Holland at the time the new colony was decided on. It was of course impossible for all to go, as money was not plentiful and the trip was expensive. So they selected the young and strong members of the church as best fitted to withstand the hardships which lay ahead.

In due time all arrangements were complete, and the hour for starting arrived. It was a sad farewell that separated these brave and fearless people. Kneeling down together for the last time, they prayed that God would keep from danger those that stayed and those that went.

Miles Standish

In July, 1620, this band of brave Pilgrims left the port of Delft Haven on the vessel *Speedwell*. Another vessel, the *Mayflower*, with friends from England was waiting for them at Plymouth. When they arrived in England they found that the *Speedwell* was too shaky to undertake the voyage, so all went on board the *Mayflower* and sailed for the New World.

There were just one hundred and two men, women,

and children in this company. Among them were many brave men, such as John Carver, William Brewster, William Bradford, and a soldier by the name of Miles Standish. This soldier was not a Pilgrim. Like John Smith, he loved adventure; and so sincerely did he admire the pluck and perseverance of the Pilgrims that he volunteered to go with them and help them.

The trip across the ocean was long and wearisome. Storms came up, and the poor people had to remain below deck most of the time. The frail vessel was so tossed by the winds and waves that it seemed as if they would never see land again.

At last after many weary weeks they saw the American coast stretched out before them; and on a bleak, wintry day, they rounded the end of Cape Cod and sailed into what is now called Provincetown Harbor. You can hardly imagine with what hope and yet with what fear they gazed at the snow-laden trees, the bare coasts, and the dark skies above.

It was while the *Mayflower* was lying at anchor in this bay that the Pilgrims drew up a written agreement in the cabin of the ship. In this agreement it was stated that all were to have equal rights; that they would live in peace and help and defend one another in time of need. They elected John Carver governor and agreed to obey such laws as should seem necessary later on.

For a month they sailed along the coast of Massachusetts Bay, endeavoring to find a suitable place to land. Oftentimes parties explored the shore in a shallop or small boat which they had brought in the

Mayflower. But Miles Standish, who usually had charge of these expeditions, preferred traveling inland to see what kind of land this bleak country was.

On more than one occasion he and his men saw Indians. One day they found several mounds, which proved to be Indian graves. A short distance away they discovered a mound freshly covered over with sand. They removed the sand and found several baskets of corn with yellow, blue, and red kernels. They were overjoyed and took the corn back with them to the ship. Later, when the Pilgrims found to whom this corn belonged, they paid the Indians for it.

During these days Miles Standish proved a very useful friend to the Pilgrims, and it was he who finally chose the spot for the colonists to land upon.

It was on the 21st of December, when the ground was knee-deep with snow and the weather biting cold, that the Pilgrims left the vessel to make their new home in this place, which John Smith had already called Plymouth.

The water was so shallow at this point that even the shallop could not quite reach the shore. Near the water's edge a large bowlder was lying, and this rock the Pilgrims used as a stepping-stone from their small boat to the dry land. To-day if you should go to Plymouth, you would see among many curious relics of the Pilgrims this interesting rock.

A large log house was hastily constructed, in which they all could live until they were able to build separate homes for each family. A platform also was put up, and

Reading the Compact in the Cabin of the "Mayflower"

on it were placed the cannon which the colonists had brought with them. It was necessary to be well armed in this strange land of savage Indians; and the colonists had come with guns, powder, and bullets for each man, and cannon for the common protection.

The "Mayflower" in Plymouth Harbor

As the winter advanced, the Pilgrims suffered great hardships. Food was getting scarce. They had used up most of the provisions brought from England. The men were nearly worn out by the heavy work they were doing. Great trees had to be hewn down and dragged to the spot where they were to be used in building. Then came the work of cutting them into the proper size and shape, and all this in bitter cold weather.

No wonder that with all these hardships so many became ill and died. Those who remained well and strong—and there were only a few of them—nursed the sick. The large log house was turned into a hospital. When spring came, only fifty were left of the one hundred and two who had sailed from England.

In order that the Indians might not know to what a small number they had been reduced, the settlers buried their dead at night and leveled the graves so that they would not be noticed.

Yet, despite the hard winter, when the *Mayflower* returned to England in the spring, not one person cared to go back. Liberty with all its hardships was sweeter than life in their old home.

One day an Indian came into the village of Plymouth and called to the people in English, "Welcome Englishmen!" His name was Samoset, and he had learned a little English from fishermen on the Maine coast. He stayed over night and left the next morning.

Shortly afterwards Samoset returned with another Indian called Squanto. Years before, Squanto had been stolen by some Englishmen and had been taken to England where he had learned to like the comforts and ways of his captors. He told the Pilgrims that the chief of his tribe, Massasoit, was coming to visit them. In an hour's time Massasoit came with sixty followers. The Pilgrims received him with all possible show. They marched to meet him, carrying their guns and beating all the drums they could muster. The chief seemed much pleased, and a peace compact was drawn up. This peace was kept for over fifty years between these Indians and the English.

Squanto afterwards came and lived in Plymouth and proved a valuable friend. He taught the English the way to plant corn, peas, and barley, and acted as interpreter between them and the neighboring tribes in their fur trading.

When spring came, the Pilgrims grew more hopeful. They had twenty acres of corn and six of barley and peas planted, and this promised a splendid harvest. With the autumn the promise was fulfilled. When they had gathered their first harvest, the Pilgrims found themselves well supplied with grain for the coming winter.

Unlike many people, they did not forget who the Giver of all this bounty was. They set aside one day for a thanksgiving for the harvest; and then, thinking the best way to show their gratitude was to give pleasure to others, they invited Massasoit and ninety of his Indians to join them in a celebration. Massasoit brought five deer for the feast. The Pilgrims themselves had sent men out to shoot wild turkey. For three days these friendly neighbors passed the time in feasting and outdoor games. From this happy beginning has grown our national custom of observing a Thanksgiving Day in the fall of each year.

Not all the Indians, however, were as friendly to the whites as were Massasoit and his tribe.

One day Canonicus, the chief of a tribe hostile to Massasoit, sent a bundle of arrows wrapped in a snake skin to Miles Standish. This was a sign of war. Standish was a brave man and did not fear the threat. He kept the arrows and, filling the snake skin with powder, returned it to Canonicus. This was enough. Canonicus thought it best to leave the English alone.

Again, Massasoit told the Pilgrims of a plot the Massachuseuks tribe was forming to kill all the English in Plymouth. Grateful for the news, Miles Standish decided to hunt up his enemies before they attacked his people. Taking a company of men with him, he fell upon the Massachuseuks and killed their leader, Pecksuot, and many others. Pecksuot had boasted the night before that he did not fear Standish because he was a little man, and he, Pecksuot, a man of great strength and courage.

The March of Miles Standish against the Massachuseuks

As the months passed, the Pilgrims were becoming more and more settled. Starting with only the large log cabin which they had built when they first landed, they had now quite a village of separate houses for the different families.

111

These log houses were not like our houses of to-day. The tiny windows were covered with oiled paper instead of glass, which was too expensive. Instead of dividing the house into dining room, kitchen, and parlor, the Pilgrims had one big room. The cooking was done over the fire under the large chimney. They had scarcely any furniture. Instead of comfortable chairs and beds, they had blocks of wood covered with the furs of wild animals. In one corner stood the large spinning wheel on which the mother and daughters spun yarn for the family use.

Governor Carver's Chair and a Colonial Spinning Wheel

The church which these people attended was simple and crude like their homes. Never safe from the Indians, the Pilgrims, even on Sunday, would march to church with their guns over their shoulders.

The life of the Pilgrim children was a busy and yet a happy one. Both boys and girls had to help their parents in the daily toil. Then they had their schools to attend. The schoolhouses were built of clumsy logs with a roof of dried grass and seaweeds. Inside, the walls were bare. There were no pictures and maps to help the children understand their lessons. The teachers were exceedingly strict and thought it wrong for children ever to waste time in play.

On Sunday the children had to walk very quietly to church, and to sit perfectly still through the reading of a sermon which was sure to last one hour, and often lasted two.

A Pilgrim Meeting House and Fort

At night they sat around the fire while their father read the Bible to all his family; and then they went to bed. If by chance they should lie awake, they were pretty sure to hear the howling of the hungry wolves which prowled about outside. It was a dreary sound.

And so passed the days and nights of the Pilgrim children, until they grew to be God-fearing men and women, honored to this day for the part they took in the first New England colony.

X

GOVERNOR WINTHROP
AND THE PURITANS

The Puritans Come to America

THE chances of sending letters from Plymouth to England were very few in the early days of that settlement. Still the Pilgrims occasionally found an opportunity to write to their friends who were left behind in England, telling of their new life in the new land.

They wrote about the hardships they had to endure, the dangers from Indians and wild beasts, and the risk of starvation. And yet one great blessing they never forgot to mention. That was their liberty to worship God as they saw fit.

Now the Pilgrims were not the only people who did not agree with all the forms of the Church of England. There were others, who, while not leaving the church, wished to have the service more simple. As they expressed it, they wanted "to purify" the church. They were called Puritans.

In the early days of the Pilgrim settlement, the

Puritans in England were having much the same trouble in carrying out their religious ideas, that the Pilgrims had undergone. And it did not take them many years to decide to follow their Pilgrim friends to America, where they, too, could have freedom of worship.

The first little party of Puritans to leave England called their American settlement Salem, a name which means "peace." A charter was granted the Salem colonists, but under its conditions the settlement was really governed from England. There the governor stayed and sent his orders to a deputy governor, who lived in the colony.

John Winthrop

Many difficulties would naturally arise from such an arrangement. Still the Puritans in England could not help being strongly tempted to follow the Salem settlers. Finally twelve leading Puritans met and determined to lead a great migration to America on the condition that the colonists could take their charter with them and be governed by a governor living in New England.

All this was agreed to, and John Winthrop was appointed governor of the Puritans already in New

England and of those who should sail with him. Of these last, there were over seven hundred. Many of them were from families of education and rank; and all were earnest, courageous, and sincere. They had eleven good ships to carry them and their horses, cattle, and other supplies.

It was in March, 1630, that they bade farewell to England. In June they reached the Massachusetts coast.

The Chief Settlements Made in New England between 1620 and 1675

A very different reception awaited the Puritans from that which had greeted the Pilgrims. Even Nature was doing her best. In place of the barren, snow-covered land, which seemed to frown upon the landing of the Pilgrims, bright flowers and green trees now nodded and waved a cheerful greeting.

No friend or foe had broken the deep silence of the forests for the Pilgrims. The Puritans found the cordial, hearty welcome of a splendid dinner served by their old friends in Salem.

However, these Puritans were not well pleased with Salem and soon moved to Charlestown. Here, they had the same terrible misfortune which seems to have come to nearly all the young American colonies. A dreadful sickness broke out and caused the death of many who were not strong enough to stand the great change in conditions.

During all the suffering, Governor Winthrop proved himself most worthy of the trust the colonists had in him. He, himself, was not spared grief. His eldest son was drowned in an attempt to swim across a channel. The Governor hid his own sorrows and went among the people and cheered them by bright hopes of the future.

At last the settlers concluded that their troubles were due to the impure water of Charlestown, and that they must make another move. They found a new locality, which they called Tri-Mountain, that suited them better. Here, they would have plenty of fresh water and a beautiful spot upon which to build their homes.

Life in Boston

IT did not take the Puritans long to build a new town. They erected a church, divided their town into lots and streets, and laid in stores of grain for the coming winter. This town they named Boston.

When the Governor had built his new home, he sent to England for the rest of his family to join him. The future was full of promise.

Then the summer days grew shorter; and, as the autumn leaves were falling, the people realized that their food supply was nearly at an end. They had used all their corn and were forced to make flour of the acorn. Instead of fresh game, they had to be satisfied with clams and crabs. And with the cold, bleak winds of winter came still more suffering and famine.

A ship had long before been sent to England for fresh supplies. In vain the men would go down to the shore and strain their eyes, eagerly scanning the horizon. But they could see no signs of the longed-for vessel.

A touching story is told of the Governor, which shows how loving and kind he was to his people. One day a poor, half-starved man came to him and begged for a morsel of bread. The Governor had only one loaf left; but, seeing that the man needed it more than he did, he gave it to him. On that very day the vessel with fresh supplies arrived from England.

And many other like acts were done by Governor

Winthrop. When a man once came to him and complained that a certain neighbor was stealing his wood, Governor Winthrop appeared very angry and said, "Does he so? I'll take a course with him. Go call that man to me. I'll warrant you I'll cure him of stealing."

The poor thief came, trembling and frightened. The Governor looked him over, saw how poor he appeared, and said, "Friend this is a very hard winter. I doubt you were but meanly provided with wood, wherefore I would have you help yourself at my wood pile till this cold season be over." And there was no more complaint of the man's stealing wood.

In his home, too, Governor Winthrop did all he could to set a good example to the colonists. Heartily disapproving of intemperance, he would allow no wine to be served at his table and tried to dissuade others from serving it.

By this time Boston was growing to be a large town. At the end of a year a thousand immigrants had arrived from England.

As the colony grew, it was necessary to have laws by which to govern the people. These laws were very strict. So were the Puritan leaders who enforced them. They ruled the people in a religious rather than a political way and saw that they kept, not only the laws of the State, but also the laws of the church. Only church members were allowed to vote.

Even the daily life of the settlers was lived according to rule. Sharply at nine every night a bell rang out the curfew, and all had to go at once to bed. At half-past four in the morning another bell warned the people that it was time to be up and doing.

Twice each Sunday every one must attend church. During service the men sat on one side of the church, and the women on the other. The little girls sat on low stools at their mothers' feet. The boys sat together, either in a pew or on the pulpit steps.

Colonial Punishment—The Stocks

And there was the tithingman, too, "to watch over youths of disorderly carriage and see they behave themselves comelie, and use such raps and blows as are in his discretion meet." This tithingman had a long stick with a hare's foot on one end and a hare's tail on the other. If a boy nodded during the long sermon, he was either tickled with the tail or rapped with the foot. His punishment depended on whether it was his first offense or a bad habit.

Many of the bad habits of the Puritans were severely punished in these early colonial days. A cross, scolding woman was made to stand outside her door with a stick tied in her mouth. A man who was caught telling an untruth had to stand in some public place with a large sign hung from his neck. On the sign was plainly printed the word "liar." The same kind of punishment was given a thief.

Culprits in the Pillory

The settlers of Boston were a very busy people. There were no stores where they could buy what they wanted, and supply-ships from England were too uncertain to be depended upon. If a housekeeper wanted linen or woolen cloth, she must weave it. If her family needed mittens or stockings, she must first spin the yarn and then knit them. Nor must she neglect making the candles and soap.

No market supplied the town with fish and meat. Each man must hunt and catch what his family were to have. He must till the soil, raise crops, and make most of the furniture and even many of the dishes for his home. And all this, after he had built the house itself, with the help of his neighbors.

This helping of one's neighbors was a noted virtue among the first colonists. When a new settler came to the colony, the men had a "chopping-bee," "a stump pulling," and a "raising"; and in no time his land was cleared and his house built. Or, if a man's crops were too heavy for him to handle alone, his neighbors fell to with a will and, for pay, wanted only his thanks.

Chair and Cradle Used in the Early Colony

It was the same with the women. They helped one another in house cleaning, rag-carpet making, and all the hard work; they visited and cared for the colony's sick, carrying them dainty dishes and nursing them back to health.

And yet with all their loving kindness, these good people had one big fault. Like the King from whom they had fled, they would allow no one to worship in any way but their way.

A young man by the name of Roger Williams soon found this out. Because of his religious opinions these hospitable, generous colonists forced him to leave their town in the dead of winter. Thanks to the help of Governor Winthrop, no serious harm befell him.

This wise and generous Governor served his colony until 1649, when he died. In the city of Boston there stands to-day a statue of John Winthrop to testify that his faithful services to the early Puritans were appreciated, not only by them, but by those who came after them.

XI

ROGER WILLIAMS

In 1631 an earnest young Puritan named Roger Williams sailed from England for Massachusetts. He became a minister at Salem.

It was true that the Puritans had left England to worship God as they wished. And they had had a great deal to say about the King's trying to make people worship only as he worshiped. But once settled in America, their leaders did just the same thing. They ordered the colonists to attend the Puritan Church, and those who were not church members could not vote.

Now, Roger Williams soon saw that this was not at all the freedom the colonists should have. He believed that a man could vote just as well if he did not belong to the church. So he said, and so he preached.

Moreover, Roger Williams told the colonists that they had no real right to the land where they were living. They replied that they had, because their charter granted it to them. That made no difference, Williams insisted; the land belonged to the Indians, and no English company had a right to give it away, and no English colonists had a right to live on it until the Indians had been paid.

It was very alarming to the Puritan leaders to have Williams spreading such notions among the settlers. What was to be done about it? The good Puritan fathers held a council and told Williams to retract. Still "he stood fast in his rocky strength." The council then ordered him to leave the colony, but allowed him to remain till spring, "if he did not go about to draw others to his opinion."

Williams still preach-ed his views. This could not go on, so a policeman was sent to arrest him. He had fled.

Thus in the dead of winter, Roger Williams became an exile in the desolate forests. For weeks he traveled through the snow, sleep-ing under any shelter he could find and living on

*Monument of
Roger Williams,
Providence, Rhode Island*

parched corn, acorns, and roots. At last he reached the Indian tribe of which Massasoit was chief; and the friendly old Indian received him as a brother and fed and cared for him.

Still he was within the boundaries of Massachusetts, and the Puritans would not have him there. He was warned to leave. So, buying from the Indians a tract of land on the shore of Narragansett Bay, Williams went to live where he would no longer be bothered by his enemies. He named his new land Providence "for God's providence to him in his distress."

Roger Williams Received by the Narragansett Indians

However, by banishing Roger Williams the Puritans did not end their troubles. There were other people left in the colony who were "like Roger Williams or worse."

One of these was Mrs. Anne Hutchinson. Her ideas were not unlike Williams's; and she, likewise, insisted on spreading them. Then she, too, must be banished; and so must her friends who agreed with her. In accord with this decision, Mrs. Hutchinson and a goodly number of her friends left their Massachusetts homes and followed Roger Williams.

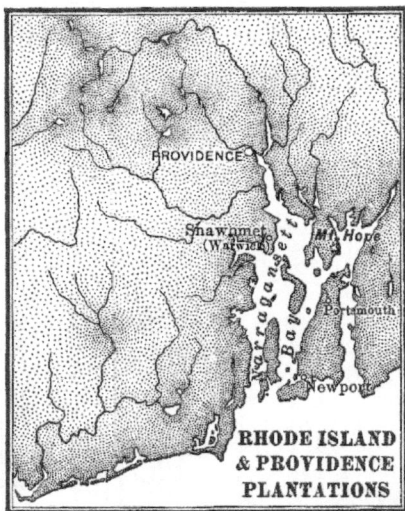

RHODE ISLAND & PROVIDENCE PLANTATIONS

The Indians gave the exiles the beautiful tract of land called Rhode Island. And there, a little later, was established a colony where, in very truth, each man could believe and worship according to his heart's desire.

For a while after this, the Puritans had no serious disturbances. Their next trouble came in a different way. A fierce war-loving Indian tribe, the Pequots, proved hostile to the Massachusetts settlers. They feared that the settlers would spread out and out and soon take all their land. This they did not mean to have, so they tried in every way to stir up the Narragansetts to join them in a massacre of the Massachusetts colonists.

Here was Roger Williams's chance to show that he was willing to practice what he preached. Although he could not agree with the Puritans, he held no grudge against them because they had refused to listen to him and had turned him out. Going to the Narragansett Indians, Williams urged them not to join the Pequots; and so great was his influence that they refused to fight.

The Pequots, nothing daunted, determined to attack

the settlers without outside aid. They did not come out in open battle, but waylaid a party of whites and killed thirty of them.

This must be stopped. So a small party of English, with a large number of friendly Indians advanced on the Pequots. Before sunrise one spring morning in 1637, the English approached the Pequots' stronghold. All were asleep. Before the Indian sentries knew what had happened, the foe was in their midst. The fort was set on fire. Only five Indians escaped, while more than four hundred perished. The great Pequot tribe was crushed, and nearly forty years of peace ensued. How different might have been the result, but for the forgiving spirit of Roger Williams!

House of the First Governor of Rhode Island

XII

KING PHILIP'S WAR

In 1675, war broke out once more between the Massachusetts settlers and the Indians. This was called King Philip's War.

King Philip was the chief of the Wampanoag tribe. His father, Massasoit, had been very friendly to the English. Philip, however, did not inherit his love for the settlers. Far from it.

There were three main reasons why King Philip looked with suspicion on the white men. The first was because of what befell his brother Alexander. On the death of Massasoit, Alexander had been made chief of the tribe. For some offense, the English had

The Indian King Philip

arrested, imprisoned, and tried him. And while in their prison, Alexander had taken a sickness which caused his death. This was hard to forgive. Why should the Englishmen interfere in the affairs of an Indian chief?

Philip's second grudge against the settlers arose from jealousy. He saw them rapidly becoming powerful and occupying large tracts of land. The land had been paid for, it is true. Yet no Indian could enjoy being shut out of his old hunting grounds that they might be turned into fields for the crops and cattle of strangers.

Indians Surprising a Settlement

In the third place, certain of these Englishmen were teaching the Indians a new religion. Many Indians had accepted the Christian faith. They were living in Christian towns and wearing the white man's clothes. "Praying Indians," they were called. What possible reason could the white man have for converting the savages unless it was to add to his own power through their friendship?

King Philip felt all these things very keenly, and yet it is doubtful if he would have gone to war over them had it not been for the urging of his warriors.

These warriors loved the warpath. For many years they had been living peacefully. Now they craved the excitement of lying in ambush and springing out on their foes; or of creeping unseen, nearer and nearer a sleeping village, and in an hour's time, turning it into a mass of flames.

So, urged on by his braves and his own inclinations, King Philip began sending messengers to friendly tribes, inviting them to join in a mighty war on "the palefaces."

The English did not know that Philip was preparing for war till an Indian told the Governor of Plymouth. For doing so, this Indian was murdered by some of Philip's men. And these, in their turn, were hanged by the English.

This was the crisis. The Indian chief's patience was at an end. These English must not hang his braves. Philip was very angry and vented his wrath on the town of Swanzey. The war that followed was a terrible one. The settlers were in constant fear and danger. Hiding behind bushes and trees, the Indians let fly their death-dealing arrows. Many of the Indians used guns, which they had secured in trade from the white men.

Oftentimes King Philip's braves, coming upon a house where a mother and her children were alone, would kill them and then burn the house. Imagine how the father must have felt when he came home from the fields and found that his whole family had been murdered! Imagine how the children must have trembled in their beds when they heard the war whoops of the approaching Indians! These savages often danced like fiends around their victims' houses, yelling and waving their tomahawks. Often a whole village would be burned to the ground, and the inhabitants killed or made captives.

First, the settlements in southern Massachusetts were attacked. Then the Indians' fury was turned on those along the western frontier. On Sunday, the 1st of September, the greater part of Deerfield was burned, only a large storehouse being saved.

During services on that same Sunday, the people of Hadley were startled to hear the yells of Indians. Seizing their guns, which were always near them, the men rushed from the church. The village seemed fairly to swarm with painted savages. For a moment all was confusion. Suddenly a man with white hair and a long white beard rushed among the terrified English. Rallying them, he led a charge against the Indians and soon put them to flight. Then the brave old fighter disappeared as suddenly as he had come.

Who was he and where did he come from? Many thought an angel had come down to deliver them from their hated foe. But the old man was merely an Englishman named William Goffe. When King Charles I of England was beheaded, this William Goffe had had a hand in the affair. He had fled to New England for protection and was at this time being secreted in the neighborhood of Hadley.

As the cold weather drew near, King Philip gathered his warriors and joined the Narragansett tribe that they might camp together during the winter. The winter was not favorable to the Indians' mode of attack. The leafless trees did not provide a good screen. So these two Indian tribes chose a piece of rising ground in the middle of a great cedar swamp, and here they fortified

Goffe Rallying the Men of Hadley

themselves. Around their camp they built a thick wall of logs. Inside the wall they set up their wigwams, and then nearly three thousand Indians settled down for the winter in what seemed to them perfect safety.

Now was the white men's chance to strike a blow that the Indians would feel. The different settlements sent men, until a goodly army was ready to march against the Indian encampment.

An Indian Palisaded Village

On the 19th of December, this army arrived at the cedar swamp. There was but one entrance to the fort, and but one way to reach the entrance. This was by crossing a brook on a fallen tree. The danger of such a crossing was plain. Still there was no hesitation. The soldiers rushed toward the log.

In an instant the walls of the fort were alive, and the front rank fell before the first blaze of the Indian guns.

135

Others sprang to take their places and were met by another volley. But nothing stopped the forward rush of the colonists. On they went, faster than the Indians could reload their guns. Crossing the log in spite of the firing, they rushed through the entrance into the fort.

A hand-to-hand fight followed. Thinking of their murdered wives and children, the white men fought like tigers. The confusion was terrible.

About sunset a blinding snowstorm filled the air; and under its protection, King Philip, the Narragansett chief, and many warriors, climbed the fortifications and fled into the forests. Then the wigwams were set on fire; and the white men retreated with their wounded and captives, leaving the Indian women and children to die in the flames with the wounded braves.

A Block-House or Pioneer Fort

In this battle over a thousand Indians perished, and the power of the mighty Narragansett tribe was completely broken.

Still, the sad fate of so many braves only added to the hate of those warriors who had escaped. The war went on as savagely as ever all through the next summer. At last King Philip's wife and son were taken prisoners. This was a hard blow for the poor chief. "Now my heart breaks," he said, "and I am ready to die."

But though he may have been ready to die, he

certainly was not ready to make peace. When one
of his warriors, discouraged by their small numbers,
suggested peace to him, Philip promptly struck the
man dead.

The Death of King Philip

Near by stood the brother of the murdered man.
In an instant, all his loyalty to his chief was turned to
hate. He would be revenged. At the first opportunity he
slipped away and going to the English told them that

they would find King Philip at his old home, Mount Hope.

And there on August 12th the avenger led a company of English soldiers, who surrounded the Indian chief before he suspected their presence. Suddenly hearing footsteps, Philip sprang to his feet and dashed for the woods. As he was fleeing past his betrayer, he received full in his heart the shot of the angry Indian. He fell on his face with his gun under him. Then his slayer sprang upon the body and chopping off the head carried it in triumph to the English colony at Plymouth. And this was the end of King Philip's War, and of the great tribe of the Wampanoag Indians.

XIII

HENRY HUDSON

THE hero of this story was an Englishman. He came of a good old English family. His home was in London, and somewhere he learned to sail the seas. This much and little more is known of the early life of Henry Hudson.

When the events happened which make him stand out in history, he was already a man. And from all he dared to do, he must surely have been a brave, persevering man at that.

For a hundred years and more explorers of the new continent had been crossing and recrossing the Atlantic. And now colonists from England, Spain, Portugal, and France were following in their path to find new homes in America.

Important as the new land was, however, it could not claim all the attention of the commercial world. There was still the wealth of India, China, and Japan to be considered. If only these countries could be quickly reached by sea! Surely there must be some route shorter than sailing around the Cape of Good Hope or through the Straits of Magellan. There must be some other possible way of sending to the East ships filled with European products—ships that would come back loaded with savory teas, coffees, and spices. Such a route must be found.

But where to find it? That was the great question. Did it lie through the new continent or did it lie around the north of Europe? This last chance offered hopes of the shorter journey and therefore must be tried.

So reasoned the Dutch, so reasoned the English, and so reasoned England's navigator, Henry Hudson. And because of this reasoning, the first years of the seventeenth century twice saw him set sail for the north.

Many were the thrilling adventures which Hudson and his men had on these two trips. No one had been so near the North Pole as they, and no one knew the dangers of arctic travel better than they. On each voyage Hudson tried a different course, but both failed to lead him where he wanted to go. Still he was not discouraged. He firmly believed there must be some passage lying up there to the north.

Henry Hudson

In Holland at this time there was a famous company known as the Dutch East India Company. In spite of all the difficulties in their way, this company had continually sent their ships to the East by way of the Cape of Good Hope. And now they were fast securing for Holland a monopoly of the Eastern trade in the desired teas, coffees, and spices. Even with the risks and expense of the long trip the company's profits were great. Think what they would be if only a short passage were found!

It is easy to see that, with their trade already established, the Dutch had a special reason for wanting to discover such a route. The Dutch East India Company believed with Hudson that the shortest way to reach China was to sail north. So, although Hudson had twice failed, the Dutch East India Company urged him to make another effort, and this time to sail under their colors. This he agreed to do. And in 1609, the year following his second voyage, he went to Holland.

On April 4th, he set sail on the Zuyder Zee in a little Dutch ship named the *Half Moon*.

A month later Hudson rounded the North Cape. But now trouble began. The sea was full of great blocks of ice. The cold was intense. It was hard to make any headway. Soon the sailors grew frightened and refused to go on. What was to be done under such conditions?

Now, it happened that Captain John Smith and Henry Hudson were great friends; and not long before, John Smith had written to Hudson from Virginia of an effort he himself had made to find a passage across the new continent. He had sailed up Chesapeake Bay and proved that there was no passage that way. Still he thought there might be one farther to the north. Thus he had written Hudson.

If there were a route to India to the north of Chesapeake Bay, why should not Hudson go in search of it, as long as his sailors would not sail any farther in the direction they had started?

Fired with this new plan, Hudson turned his ship about and headed for America. On July 18th, the little *Half Moon* reached Penobscot Bay, much the worse for wear. Here a short time was spent in repairing the damages done by the rough seas, and then with all sails spread Hudson set out to follow the American coast toward the south.

Slowly he sailed along, always on the lookout for some sign of the passage he sought, and little dreaming that the continent he skirted stretched fully three thousand miles to the west. On went the Dutch vessel until Hudson judged, and correctly too, that he must be off the shores of Virginia. There was no chance of finding what he sought here, according to John Smith; so once more the *Half Moon* was turned about and headed north.

The 3d of September was a clear, bright day. The blue sky, the gleaming waves, the swaying green forests along the coast, made a picture not to be forgotten. The little Dutch ship scudded along in the sunshine, while, from her bow, Henry Hudson watched the wide-spreading shores of a bay which opened just ahead. Might not this opening be the passage to the Pacific? Surely everything pointed that way. With his heart full of hope, the brave navigator ran his ship into the bay and dropped anchor.

The "Half Moon" in the Highlands of the Hudson

Then out from the shore glided light canoes. Their red-faced owners paddled nearer and nearer the strange-looking "great white bird," as they called the white-sailed ship. Slowly the canoes circled round and round the *Half Moon*. At last, seeing no signs of danger, the Indians came close to the ship. Leaning over its side, Hudson politely asked the red men to come aboard.

After this first visit, the Indians came again and brought grapes, furs, pumpkins, and tobacco, which they gave the sailors for some knives and beads.

A few days later the *Half Moon* was again under sail, and Henry Hudson was cautiously making his way up the great river which now bears his name. All along the shores the red faces of curious Indians peered out through the trees. Some were friendly and glad to see the strange ship. Others shot arrows at the sailors.

Near the present site of Catskill a cordial old chief asked Hudson to go ashore. In the old chief's bark home Hudson was served with a great feast of wild pigeons and a fine dog, which was killed, skinned, and roasted while the guest waited. After the feast Hudson rose to return to his ship. The Indians were disappointed. They wanted the white man to stay until morning. How could they show him that he had nothing to fear? Suddenly one of their number jumped up, gathered all the arrows, and, breaking them in pieces, threw them on the fire. Hudson was touched by the act, but nevertheless did not accept the cordial invitation to remain.

The Indians Beg Hudson To Stay with Them

By the time Hudson had sailed as far as Albany, the hope that he had found a water way to the Pacific had gradually faded away. Bitterly disappointed at finding the water growing so shallow that he feared to run his ship aground, he turned back and put to sea again. This was Henry Hudson's only visit to the Hudson River.

Many of Hudson's sailors, as well as the commander himself, being Englishmen, the temptation to land at an English port was too great to resist. On November 7th, the *Half Moon* arrived at Dartmouth, England. And from England, Hudson sent his report on to the Dutch East India Company in Holland. He told all the details of his voyage; still asserted that there must be a northwest way to reach India, and asked for more money and fresh sailors with which to make a new start in the spring.

The Dutch East India Company read the report most carefully, and then they sent for Hudson to meet them and talk the matter over.

But no! The English King would not listen to Hudson's sailing again for the Dutch. If he could find a northwest route to the East, he should find it for England—not for Holland. So the little *Half Moon* was sent off home. And in April, 1610, Henry Hudson left England in an English ship for one more trial at reaching India.

Sailing farther north than on his last voyage, Hudson this time entered the landlocked water which has ever since been called Hudson Bay.

By the middle of November, his ship was frozen hard and fast in the ice. It was dreadfully cold, food was growing scarce, and the sailors were wishing they had stayed at home.

All winter and until the 18th of the next June the ice held. When it finally broke, the crew were determined to return to England at once. Hudson was just as determined to push on toward the west. All held firmly to their own opinion. The crew would not sail west, and Hudson would not turn back.

There was only one commander, and there were many sailors. So, being the stronger, the crew solved the question in their own way. Three days after the ice gave way they put Hudson, his son, and several sick men into the ship's open boat and set them adrift. Then the ship was faced about for home.

What became of Henry Hudson, what hardships he suffered, and how long his little open boat lived among the great blocks of floating ice, are things that will never be known. But it is doubtless true that the brave English mariner went down sooner or later in the icy waters of Hudson Bay.

XIV

THE DUTCH IN AMERICA

Peter Minuit

AFTER Henry Hudson had crossed the ocean and explored the river now called by his name, Dutch interest in the New World awakened. Dutch merchants grew eager to trade with the natives of this new country when once they had seen the beautiful furs which Hudson had brought back in the *Half Moon*.

So, as the years went by, Dutch ships appeared at the mouth of the Hudson; and traders from Holland offered the Indians blue glass beads and strips of red cotton for beaver, otter, and mink skins. A few rough huts were built on the Indian island of Manhattan and were used both as a shelter and as a trading post. The neighboring country was explored, and to all this region the Dutchmen gave the name of New Netherland.

In 1618 these enterprising traders built a fort or strong house not far from the present site of Albany. Here they set up a few cannon and established a small garrison. Then the commander of the little company did a thing which was to prove a lasting good to many people for many years. He invited the chiefs of all the powerful Iroquois Indian tribes to hold a conference with him.

Old Dutch Fort

They came gladly. With great solemnity the peace pipe was passed around, and both Dutch and Indians smoked it. Next, a hard-and-fast agreement was made between them. The Indians were to bring all their furs to the Dutch traders and in return were to receive powder and muskets. Finally, as a sign of lasting peace, a tomahawk was buried, over which the Dutch were to build a church, so that it could not be dug up and the treaty ruined. This was the great treaty of Tawasentha.

A little later there was formed in Holland a company known as the Dutch West India Company, and in 1623 this Dutch West India Company sent a colonizing expedition to New Netherland. Thirty families sailed under the leadership of Cornelius May, who was elected their first governor.

A good deal seems to have been expected from these thirty families in the way of settlements. There were only one hundred and ten people in all, and a village of one hundred and ten people is a pretty small town. So you can picture how large their towns must have been when one hundred and ten were divided into several different settlements.

Some of the families stayed on Manhattan Island and built themselves cozy little Dutch homes.

In 1626 Peter Minuit was appointed Governor of New Netherland and came to the Manhattan settlement. He was one of the best and wisest governors that the Dutch West India Company ever sent to look after their interests in America.

Now, up to this time the Dutch had lived on the island of Manhattan without questioning whether it was right or wrong

The Dutch and Neighboring Settlements

for them to do so. When Peter Minuit came, he said that the island belonged to the Indians, and that they must be paid for it before the Dutch could call it their own. So he sent to the Indians inhabiting Manhattan and asked them to sell the island to him.

The Indian chiefs were willing to part with the land and sold the whole island to the Dutch for twenty-four dollars' worth of beads, ribbons, knives, and blankets. There must have been a great pile of these trinkets which the natives valued so much; and as they knew that there was plenty of land to the West, it is probable that they were well pleased with their bargain.

You see the Indians did not know the value of gold and silver money. The only money they knew or valued was what they called wampum. This wampum was made of shells or beads which had holes through them and were strung on strings. A string of colored beads would buy twice as much corn as a string of the same number of white beads.

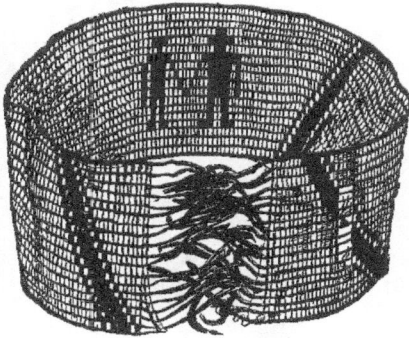

Indian Treaty Belt Wampum

Wampum was put to other uses besides that of trading. As the Indians could not write, they kept their records in beads. After a council a belt would be woven in such a way that an Indian could tell from the color and arrangement of the beads just what had been done. Treaty belts, too, were made in this way and given as a pledge that the terms of the treaty would be kept.

After Manhattan became Dutch property, Peter

Minuit built a blockhouse surrounded by strong palisades for the protection of the little town which was named New Amsterdam. During the summer more settlers came, and soon there were thirty houses in the village. Besides these houses there was a large windmill, a flagstaff from which the Dutch colors floated on the breeze, and later a church. On one side of the church was the Governor's house; on the other, the

A Dutch Windmill

prison. Fields were planted with wheat, rye, corn, barley, and oats. Meadows were laid out and stocked with cows, sheep, and goats. And the industrious Dutchmen soon felt much at home.

The Indians and the New Amsterdam settlers were on very friendly terms, and the Indians constantly came into the town to sell their furs to the white men. This trade in furs was carried on between the Indians and the fur traders of other New Netherland settlements as well as with those of New Amsterdam, and it became the great industry of the colony.

One other industry was carried on by these thrifty people. They cut down great trees from the forests and shipped the timber to Holland. When they had cut more than they could ship, they began to build vessels of their own to sail up and down the river and even to the West Indies, with which they were fast building up a trade.

And yet in spite of the shipbuilding, the profitable fur trading, and all the advantages to be had in New Netherland, the Dutch were slow in coming to America. They were too happy at home to care to leave Holland.

The Dutch West India Company saw that some new inducement must be made if their colony was to grow fast enough to suit them. So they offered a tract of land to any member of their company who would agree to have fifty colonists settled on his property within four years. Anyone accepting the offer could choose his own land along any river in the company's domain. If his estate lay on only one bank of the river, he could claim sixteen miles of shore line. Or, he could have eight miles on each bank. In either case his estate should run back from the river as far as he wished it to. The owners of these estates were to be called patroons.

The patroon must consent to pay the Indians for his land, to pay the traveling expenses of his fifty colonists, to fit them out with the necessities of farming, and to provide a schoolmaster and a minister for his estate.

In a short time five such estates were laid out, and the proprietors acted like lords. They did not need to exert themselves, for they had all the help they could desire and almost absolute power over all the settlers living on their lands.

In 1632 Peter Minuit was removed from the governorship of New Netherland and sailed away from New Amsterdam after a short but useful service.

Peter Stuyvesant

PETER STUYVESANT was the last of the Dutch governors of New Netherland. He came to the colony in 1647 and ruled for seventeen years. And they were trying years for both the people and the Governor.

Peter Stuyvesant had many good qualities and many faults. He was loyal to the company that had appointed him and tyrannical to the people he governed. He was honest, brave, and fearless. But he was hot tempered, stern, and unrelenting. His motives were good, but his methods severe.

Above all he was stubborn. So stubborn indeed that before he had been long in the colony he was nicknamed "Headstrong Peter." "Old Silverleg" was another name given him.

These two nicknames illustrate perfectly the contradictory make-up of the man. The first one was given him because of his pig-headedness. The second came through loyal service to his country. He had lost a leg in battle and now stumped about on a wooden peg trimmed with bands of silver.

Peter Stuyvesant found many trials awaiting him in New Netherland. Troublesome neighbors were on every side. Governor Kieft whom he succeeded had had no tact with the Indians. One quarrel had been settled only to be followed by another. War of course had resulted. And although the Indians had been defeated and peace again established before Peter Stuyvesant came to take Governor Kieft's place, the Indians were still restless and revengeful. They were on the lookout for trouble and had to be treated with great care.

Then south of New Netherland lay a Swedish settlement on Delaware Bay. Here trouble of another sort was waiting for the new governor. The Swedes had settled on land which the Dutch claimed was theirs; and the Swedes had been ordered to leave, but had paid no attention to the order. Instead, they had built a fort to protect themselves and had sent for more settlers. Then the Dutch had built a fort near the Swedish fort to enforce their claim. This the Swedes had torn down.

And thus it went until Peter Stuyvesant decided to settle matters once for all. So taking seven ships and seven hundred men he swooped down upon the little colony, forced it to surrender, and turned it from a Swedish to a Dutch colony.

With the English colonists to the east, Peter Stuyvesant had difficulties, too. The English had gradually occupied Connecticut; and now they were crowding the Dutch on Long Island, and even in the land between the Connecticut and Hudson rivers. Settlement of the boundary lines cost much time and many heated arguments.

View of New Amsterdam, 1651
(probably the earliest printed)

And all this while Peter Stuyvesant was having other heated arguments with his own colonists. They had many grievances against their governor. They complained of the taxes; they did not want to be controlled solely by a governor, for they themselves wanted a voice in the government.

At last they won what they asked, and Peter Stuyvesant was obliged to listen to their claims. A council of nine men was elected to confer with the Governor, and this council did much toward remedying the evils of which the people complained.

Now, although Peter Stuyvesant's rule was such a stormy one, he left the colony far better than he found it. New Amsterdam especially improved under his care. The town was given a charter and made into a city. And it was a pretty city, too. Along the streets stood the rows of quaint Dutch houses. Their gables were of colored brick and were turned toward the street; weathercocks decorated the roofs. Bright little gardens lay before many houses. And the gay-colored clothes of the people lent a cheerful appearance to the town.

A Street of New Amsterdam

In the public square stood the stocks, whipping post, and pillory for the punishment of offenders. As Governor Stuyvesant was very fond of dealing out public punishment, all three were often occupied at once. Then there was the fort built by Peter Minuit and strengthened by Peter Stuyvesant. Scattered about were Dutch windmills with their four long sweeping arms. And all together New Amsterdam was a charming little town and one of which the Dutch Governor might well be proud. But Peter Stuyvesant's pride in his colony was short-lived.

England and Holland were great commercial rivals; and England had long ago, owing to John Cabot's discoveries, claimed the land occupied by New Netherland. Moreover, the English king was determined to have all the English colonies along the Atlantic coast united, and this was impossible so long as the Dutch held New Netherland. So the English king gave the Dutch land to his brother James, the Duke of York, who sent a fleet to demand the surrender of the Dutch colony.

Suddenly one day this fleet appeared off New Amsterdam, and its commander sent a letter to Governor Stuyvesant. The letter invited him to give up his colony to the Duke of York. In return for the surrender, the colonists were to be allowed to keep their property and all their rights and privileges, and other privileges were to be granted them.

"Old Silverleg" was very wrathful. He tore up the letter and stamped about on his wooden leg swearing that he would rather be carried out dead than give up the fort. He called upon the Dutch to help him, but they refused to come to his aid, as they were anxious

Peter Stuyvesant Tearing Up the English Letter

to accept the liberal terms of the English.

Poor "Headstrong Peter" could do nothing alone; and a white flag was raised in spite of him, and the colony was given over to the English. This ended Dutch rule in America.

The name New Netherland was changed to the Province of New York in honor of the English king's brother, the Duke of York. And for the same reason New Amsterdam became the city of New York.

Sailing to Holland, Peter Stuyvesant reported the surrender to the Dutch West India Company. Then he returned to his home in New York and lived there as a peaceful citizen all the rest of his life. He died in 1682 when he was eighty years old.

Governor Stuyvesant's Country House

XV

THE EARLY FRENCH EXPLORERS

Verrazano

When Columbus discovered America, all the kings of Europe belonged to the Catholic Church and looked to the Pope at Rome as their ruler. So, when the kings of Spain and Portugal began to quarrel about lands outside their kingdoms, it was the Pope who settled their disputes. He took a map and drew upon it a line from the north pole to the south pole, three hundred and seventy leagues west of the Cape Verde Islands. All the land west of this line not belonging to some Christian prince was to belong to Spain; all east of it, to Portugal.

Now if the Pope's decision had remained final, our country would be very different from what it is to-day. Instead of being a nation of English-speaking people, it would have become a colony of Spain.

When the French king heard about this line he said, "I would like to see the clause in Father Adam's will which divides the world between the Portuguese and the Spaniards. I think France shall have a share, too."

So he began to look about for a bold seaman to make discoveries and claims for France. In 1523 he heard of a sailor by the name of Verrazano.

The French king sent for Verrazano and told him that he wanted him to go in search of a passage westward to China. Verrazano consented and in 1524 started out.

After a journey of forty-nine days the voyagers reached a low shore on the coast of what is now North Carolina. Here a glad sight met their eyes. Fires were blazing on the sandy beach. Behind were tall forests of pine, laurel, and cypress. Along the beach surprised Indians, befeathered, and almost naked, ran like deer. They gave cries of welcome to the white men and showed them where to land.

But Verrazano did not loiter long. He sailed up the coast as far north as Newfoundland. By this time his supply of food had become scanty, so he went back to France.

When Verrazano got back to France, his brother, who had been one of the voyagers, drew a queer map of the coast along which they had traveled. This map is preserved in Rome to this day. Verrazano himself wrote a long letter to the King of France. In this letter he describes the appearance and habits of the Indians, and gives a very interesting account of the trees and plants along the coast. He tells of the fur-bearing animals which he found as he sailed north.

Verrazano's Ship Nearing Newfoundland

But even before Verrazano had finished writing his letter to the King, that monarch had gone to war with Italy. He was taken prisoner, and soon France was so busy fighting with her neighbors that she had no time to think about the lands across the sea.

Jacques Cartier

IF you look at a map of France you will see on the western coast a large peninsula jutting into the sea. On a point of this peninsula is the very old and strongly built town of St. Malo. This town has always been famous for its hardy and skillful seamen.

One April day, in the year 1534, just ten years after Verrazano's voyage, the shore of St. Malo was crowded with people. They were waving a farewell to two ships that were sailing out of the harbor, bound westward. Once safely back in France after escaping from his captivity, the French King had remembered Verrazano's letter. Now he thought that it would be a fine thing to send some one over to seize the land which Verrazano had explored. And that is how the two ships happened to be sailing out of the harbor of St. Malo on that April morning of 1534. They were under the command of Jacques Cartier, the very bravest and most experienced of all the brave sailors of St. Malo.

Jacques Cartier

Before long, Cartier's ships reached the coast of Newfoundland. They passed through the Straits of Belle Isle and entered the great gulf on the coast of North America, opposite Newfoundland. Landing at Cape Gaspé, Cartier set up a cross thirty feet high. Upon this was carved, in French, the words, "Long live the King of France." This meant that Cartier claimed the land for France.

The chief of the neighboring Indians did not like the cross. When the Frenchmen had boarded their ships to start back to France, the chief, dressed in a bear's skin, came out to them in a canoe. With him were two of his sons. The chief began to complain to Cartier about the cross. He said that the land belonged to the Indians. Cartier and his men coaxed them to come close to the ship. Then several of the French sailors jumped into the canoe, and brought it alongside.

A Missionary Priest

The French took the Indians on board the ship, thus frightening them very much. But the French pretended to be friendly. They told them that the cross was set up only as a beacon or landmark by which the French could find their way back to the port. Cartier promised that he would soon come again and bring a good supply of iron kettles and other things that the Indians prized. Then he told the chief that he must let his two sons go to France. The chief did not want to let them go, but he could not help himself. To make the Indian boys more willing to go, the French sailors dressed them in gay coats and red caps and put copper chains about their necks.

When Cartier had sailed back to France, and had given the King a fine account of what he had seen, the King decided to send him upon a second voyage.

In May, 1535, Cartier sailed with three ships and over a hundred men, besides the two Indian boys whom he had kidnaped on the first voyage. In August they reached the shores of Canada.

On the day which the Catholics call "St. Lawrence's Day," Cartier's ships entered the great gulf where he had been the year before. So they named this the Gulf of St. Lawrence.

Sailing on up the river, the French came to an Indian village, called Stadaconé. This village stood on the very spot where the old rock-walled city of Quebec stands to-day. Cartier persuaded the Indians that he had come for peace. So they allowed him to moor his vessel. They told him about another Indian village, many days' journey up the river. This town, they said, was far greater than Stadaconé. It was called Hochelaga.

To Hochelaga Cartier resolved to go, in his smallest ship, with his two young Indians as guides. On they sailed, until they neared a shore swarming with Indians. The next morning these Indians guided the French through the woods to the great village they had come to see.

The travelers entered the town through the narrow gate. Within, they saw about fifty queer dwellings. Each house was fifty yards long and twelve or fifteen yards wide, and contained many fires and many families. These houses were made of poles covered with sheets of bark.

In the middle of the town was an open square. Here Cartier and his men stopped, while from the bark houses poured out crowds of men, women, and children. They came close to the visitors and felt of their beards and faces. They were trying to find out whether these strange-colored, strangely dressed beings, with gleaming guns and swords and helmets, were men or gods.

After a while the Indian warriors made the women and children go farther away, while they themselves squatted on the ground around the French. Some of the women brought mats for Cartier and his men to sit upon.

Next, a number of warriors went into one of the houses, and came out carrying upon a deerskin a very old Indian helpless with paralysis. He wore very dirty clothes, but on his straight black hair was a sort of red crown made of porcupine quills. This was the chief of the village. The Indians put him on the ground in front of Cartier and made signs of welcome for him. The poor old chief pointed at his helpless limbs and seemed to beg the French chief to touch and heal them. Cartier laid his hands upon the old man and pretended to heal him.

Then he began to distribute presents. To the women he gave beads. To the children he threw rings and other jewelry, made of tin. Then the French trumpeters put their trumpets to their lips and blew a mighty blast. This surprised and pleased the Indians very much.

The French now set forth, guided by a band of Indians, to explore the great mountain back of the village. When Cartier had climbed this mountain and looked far out upon the forests below, with the river winding like a blue ribbon between them, he gave it the name of Montreal, the French for "Royal Mountain."

Going back to their ship, the French sailed down the St. Lawrence to Stadaconé. Here they found that the Frenchmen who had stayed behind had built themselves a fort; and here Cartier and his men spent the long, severe winter, suffering great torture from cold and sickness.

A French Fur Trader

By spring the men were all well again. The ice which held the ships fast in the river melted away and set them free, and Cartier returned to France. He had discovered a mighty river and a great mountain.

The King of France heard Cartier's report and was much pleased. But trouble at home prevented him for several years from sending another expedition. When he did send it, he took men from prisons for colonists. These men made a great deal of trouble, and finally the hope of a colony was given up by the King.

Jean Ribaut

DURING the sixteenth century the Protestant faith made many converts in European countries; and because of the difference in their religious views, the Catholics and Protestants were continually at strife with one another.

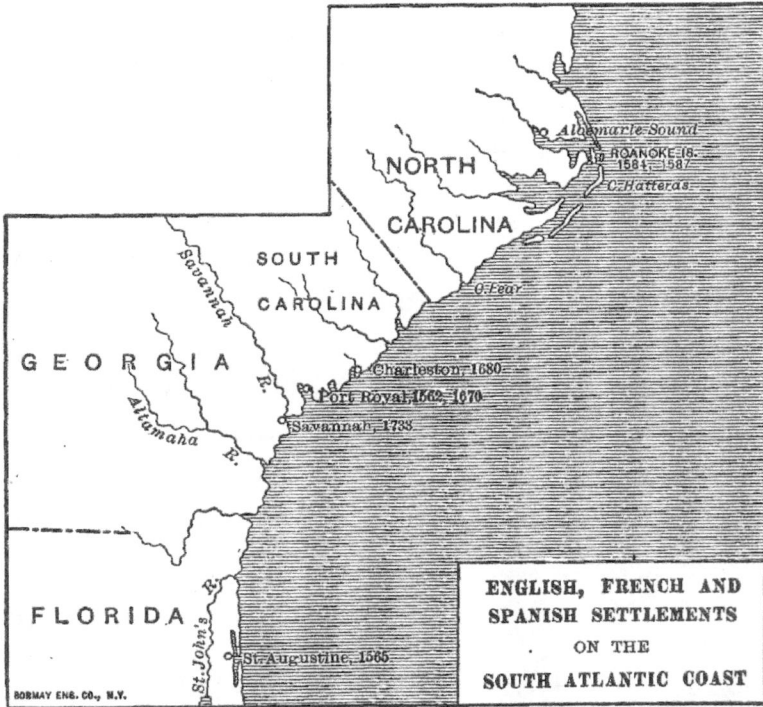

because of the difference in their religious views, the Catholics and Protestants were continually at strife with one another.

In France the Protestants were called Huguenots. Their leader was a wise and good man named Admiral Coligny. He was very unhappy at seeing the Huguenots suffering torture and death for their religion, and thought it wise to send them to America to plant a Huguenot colony. Admiral Coligny selected a good and brave Huguenot named Jean Ribaut to sail in charge of the expedition. The colony started in February, 1562. First touching the coast of Florida they sailed north to what is now the coast of South Carolina.

After a while they came to a fine harbor, which

they called Port Royal. Jean Ribaut decided to leave a colony here, while he went back to France for more men and supplies.

At first the colonists were very happy. They built a fort. They passed the winter in hunting and fishing and trading with the Indians. When spring came they began to look for Ribaut's return.

But the spring and summer passed by, with no Jean Ribaut. When autumn set in, the colonists became homesick. They had planted no crops and had to depend upon the Indians for food.

The Huguenots made up their minds to go back to France. But how? Behind them lay the dense forest. Before them lay three thousand miles of ocean. Jean Ribaut had taken both of the ships. They must build a ship for themselves. They did not know a thing about shipbuilding, but where there's a will there's a way. Ribaut had left them some iron and a forge. Some of the men began to make nails and spikes and bolts, while others cut down trees. Some gathered pitch from the pine trees. The Indians made cordage. Everyone worked with a will. Finally the vessel was built, but it had no sails. They sewed together their sheets and shirts, and with these strange sails they rigged the ship. It was the queerest-looking craft that ever sailed from a port. It was not fit to navigate a duck pond, but it started bravely forth across the great Atlantic.

A fair wind filled the sails, and for several days the strange ship floated gallantly enough toward the home land. Then a calm came, and the vessel stood "like a painted ship upon a painted ocean." Next a terrible storm gashed the sails and twisted the ungainly timbers. The voyagers had endured many hardships when finally they were picked up by an English vessel and carried prisoners to Queen Elizabeth.

But why had not Jean Ribaut come back? When he got to France war was going on as usual. Admiral Coligny could not get another expedition ready before the spring of 1564. Then three ships sailed under Captain Laudonnière. They landed at the St. John's River in Florida.

Laudonnière and his men soon built a little town. Here they lived by hunting and fishing and farming. One evening, when this colony had been in America a little more than a year, they saw ships approaching.

The next morning everyone was up by daylight. Seven large ships were sailing up the river. Their decks were filled with men in armor. The colonists called to them, but they made no answer. Laudonnière had only two cannon. He ordered these to be aimed at the ships. He was just about to give the command to fire, when the strangers called out, "We are Huguenots!"

It was true. The ships were full of men, women, and children under Jean Ribaut. You may guess how happy the colonists were.

"Now," they said, "we have come to stay." Ah, yes, they had come to stay.

The rest of the Huguenots' story is soon told. While they had been preparing to make themselves a peaceful home in the New World, the Spaniards had heard of their settlement. The King of Spain sent some soldiers to Florida, under Pedro Menendez. These soldiers made a settlement at St. Augustine, south of the Huguenot colony. Not long after Jean Ribaut came with his seven ships, the Spaniards attacked the French colony. Almost all of the Huguenots were killed, Jean Ribaut among the rest.

The Old Spanish Fort at St. Augustine

When the French king heard about this massacre, he did not seem to care. But there was a Frenchman by the name of De Gourgues, who hated the Spaniards. This De Gourgues sold all of his property and fitted out ships with the money. With some other Frenchmen he attacked the Spaniards on the St. John's and killed every one. Then he sailed back to France. He had not come to make a colony, but to take revenge upon the Spaniards for the murder of his countrymen.

XVI

CHAMPLAIN

Founding of Quebec

In the year 1603, two little French ships sailed up the St. Lawrence. Upon the deck of one of these ships stood a young and fearless-looking man, Samuel Champlain.

Past the high rock where Quebec now stands, past the broad lake of St. Peter, the ships sailed steadily on, until a high mountain rose before the voyagers. Champlain had read of Cartier's voyage, and he knew that this was the same Montreal which Cartier had explored. With his comrades Champlain landed and looked for the village of Hochelaga. It was gone, and there were only a few wandering Algonquin Indians to greet the French voyagers.

The French explorers spent the summer in looking over the country near the St. Lawrence River. When autumn came they returned to France.

The next year the two ships came again. This time the voyagers were determined to make a settlement upon the shores of the New World. First they tried a rocky island in Passamaquoddy Bay. Then they moved to a place that they named Port Royal. They spent three winters in these two places. When spring came after the third winter, it brought bad news from France. The French king would no longer support the colony in America.

With heavy hearts the colonists prepared to go home. Their Indian friends followed them to the water's edge and cried bitterly.

For a year after this, Champlain stayed in France. He grew homesick for the foggy coasts of Canada, for the sound of the sea and the smell of the pine woods. When King Henry decided to send another colony to America, there was no happier man in all France than Champlain.

Samuel de Champlain
(at about the age of sixty-five)

By the summer of 1608 a gang of choppers was at work where the city of Quebec is to-day. They were clearing a place for Champlain's new colony. The little town was soon built. It consisted of three houses and a courtyard. Around this little town was a wooden wall, and upon the inside of the wall was a gallery. In the gallery were loopholes, through which the colonists might shoot upon their enemies. Around the wall was a moat, or ditch, and near by was a garden.

The Settlement at Quebec

One morning, while Champlain was overseeing the work in the garden, one of the pilots came to him and told him that he had heard of a plot against his life. Near the French colony were some Spaniards. Some men in Champlain's colony were planning to kill him and give the colony up to the Spaniards. Champlain considered for a little while. Then he said, "I have a plan." He had a small vessel anchored in front of the town. On this boat he put a young man whom he could trust. To this man he gave two bottles of wine. "Tell the four ringleaders of the plot," he said, "that their friends have sent you some wine."

The young man told the ringleaders and invited them on board to spend the evening. As soon as they were once on the ship they were arrested. The worst one was hanged. The other three were sent to France for punishment.

When autumn came, one ship sailed for France. Champlain stayed behind with twenty-eight men.

With the cold weather, a band of roving Indians came and built their birch huts beside Champlain's colony. All winter long they did nothing but eat, and sleep on piles of branches in their smoky huts. This would have been a very happy life for them, had it not been for one thing. When they slept they dreamed fearful dreams of war with their dreaded enemies, the Iroquois. Night after night these dreams were repeated. The Indians believed that dreams were a sign of what was going to happen. They were afraid that the Iroquois were coming, and they begged the French to let them come inside the wooden walls at night. The French let the women and children come in, but they made the warriors stay outside.

The French had their difficulties as well as the Indians. Disease swept through the colony. When spring came there were only eight men left. Never was ship more welcome than the one that now arrived bearing friends and supplies from France.

The Attack on the Iroquois

CHAMPLAIN now decided that, while part of the men stayed at Quebec, he and the others would go to look for a water passage to China. The Europeans could not give up hope of finding such a passage. But what could this handful of men do among the thousands of warlike Indians scattered through the forests they must cross? Champlain thought over this for a long while. Finally he hit upon a scheme.

You remember how the Indians were frightened by their dreams about the Iroquois. The Iroquois were the fiercest and most powerful Indians in America. They were a league of five nations, living in what is now the State of New York. The other Indians east of the Mississippi belonged to the Algonquins or to the Hurons. The Iroquois hated the Algonquins and the Hurons, and oftentimes these enemies started out to make savage war against each other.

Champlain's plan was to join one of the Algonquin-Huron war parties. By doing this he would make the Algonquins and the Hurons firm friends of the French. Besides, the Algonquins had told Champlain of a great lake in the land of the Iroquois, and he was eager to see this lake.

Champlain sent for some of the Algonquins he knew, and told them that he would help them against their enemies. They soon spread the news.

A great band of warriors assembled at Quebec. Most of them had never before seen white men. They wondered at the Frenchmen's white faces, at their beards, and at their suits of steel. They stuffed themselves with the white men's food and yelled with terror at the roar of guns and cannon. They pitched their camps and got ready for the war dance.

At night, when all was still, a bright fire was built. The Indians formed a circle around this fire. Their faces were streaked with paint, and in their hands they swung stone war clubs and hatchets. Then a drum began to beat, and away they whirled in the wildest dance. After this was over they held the war feast.

It was almost July when the party started. Champlain and eleven other white men were in a small boat, each with gun and sword and armor. Around them were one hundred birch canoes full of Indians.

Champlain's Battle with the Iroquois

Swish, swish went the water, as hundreds of paddles rushed up the river. Through a lake and between islands they went, till they came to the mouth of the Richelieu River which flows into the St. Lawrence. Here they encamped. But the Indians continually quarreled with one another, until at last three-fourths of them got angry and paddled home.

Again the allies got under way—this time up the river at whose mouth they had encamped. Soon they came to a place where the river was full of rocks. No boat could cross such rapids. So nine of the white men went back to Quebec with Champlain's boat, while he and the other two went on with the Indians in their canoes.

After a time the river grew wider again, and at last they came to the great lake that the Indians had told Champlain about. He named it Lake Champlain.

The travelers now had to proceed more carefully, for they were near the home of the Iroquois. All day they would hide quietly in the woods. At night they would launch their canoes and skim over the lake.

On the night of July 29th, they started full of hope. At about ten o'clock they saw dark objects on the lake in front of them. They were the canoes of the Iroquois. Each party saw the other, and the lake rang with war cries.

The Iroquois did not like to fight on the water, so they landed and began to hack down trees for a barricade. Champlain and his party stayed on the lake and fastened their canoes together with poles.

Before daylight Champlain and the other white men put on their armor. Over their shoulders they hung their ammunition boxes; they fastened their swords to their belts and took their guns in hand. The three Frenchmen were in separate canoes. When it grew light they kept hidden under Indian robes. The canoes were pulled up close to the shore, and the Algonquin-Huron party landed, the Frenchmen hiding behind the Indians.

When two hundred of the straightest and fiercest of the Iroquois braves came marching toward them from their barricade, the Hurons and Algonquins began to feel anxious. So Champlain stepped out in front of them. The Iroquois stood

Champlain Monument in Quebec

thunderstruck. They had never seen a white man. He aimed his gun. Bang! A chief fell dead, and another rolled wounded into the bushes. Champlain's Indians gave a terrible yell, and the woods were full of whizzing arrows. For a moment the Iroquois shot back. But from among their enemies came another gunshot, and another.

They could stand it no longer. They broke rank and fled in terror through the bushes, like deer. Like hounds went the Hurons and Algonquins in hot pursuit. Some of the Iroquois were killed, many were taken prisoners. The rest ran away. Camp, canoes, provisions—all were left behind. The white man's gun had done its work.

In after years the Iroquois were always the enemies of the French, and this was only the first of many wars between them.

As the years went by, Champlain pushed farther west from Quebec. He discovered Lake Huron. He planted the French people firmly in Canada. Even to-day you will find the French language spoken in the parts of Canada which Champlain settled. His settlement at Quebec became the center, not only of military operations, but also of a large fur trade. From there, the fur traders made their way into the Indian lands and bought furs for beads, purses, and trinkets of many sorts. Much of the profits of this trade went to the King of France and much to the government of Canada.

On Christmas Day, 1635, one hundred years after Cartier had discovered the site of Montreal, there was great sadness at Quebec. The French had lost their greatest explorer, and the Indians had lost their best friend. Champlain was dead.

XVII

JOLIET AND MARQUETTE

WHEN Champlain died he left the power of the French firmly planted in Canada, which was fast becoming a famous trading post for the fur traders.

Besides the fur traders and those looking simply for adventure, there was another class of Frenchmen who came to Canada as the years went by. These were the hardest workers and bravest adventurers of all. They were the Jesuits, a society of French Roman Catholics who had sworn to do all they could to convert the world to the Catholic religion. Brave and fearless, they were eager to go into the wilds of America and make the Indians a great Catholic nation. Soon they pushed their way along the borders of the Great Lakes and established settlements, or missions, where they tried to teach and civilize the wayward red men.

At one of these missions, on Lake Superior, was a young Jesuit priest named Jacques Marquette, or Father Marquette, as he was called. Father Marquette loved the Indians and tried very hard to make them Christians. He learned to speak six different Indian languages.

Every year the Illinois Indians used to come to the

Jesuit settlement, and from them Father Marquette heard about a great river which they had to cross on their way. This river they called the "Mesipi." Father Marquette was very anxious to find this river, which he thought must flow into the Gulf of California.

At this time the Governor of Canada was Count Frontenac. Through the Indians he, too, heard about the great river; and he resolved to send some one to find it and to explore it for France. For this expedition he selected a brave young man by the name of Louis Joliet and gave him orders to take Father Marquette on the voyage.

In May, 1673, they started. They coasted along the shores of Lake Michigan until they came to a village of the Menomonies, or "wild-rice" Indians. These Indians did all they could to prevent Joliet and Marquette from going farther. "There are fierce tribes on the banks of the Mississippi who tomahawk all strangers," they said. "Besides, there is a demon in the river, who will drown you in the cave where he lives. And even if you should escape these dangers, the heat will burn you up."

But the white men were not frightened. Marquette taught the Indians a prayer and again set forth with his companions. When they came to the head of Green Bay they entered the Fox River. After paddling for several days between fields of wild rice and prairies covered with deer and elk, they came to a little hill on which was an Indian village. The Indians were friendly, and Marquette was very glad to find a cross set up hung with deerskins and red girdles and bows and arrows. These,

TERRITORY EXPLORED AND SETTLED BY THE FRENCH

the Indians said, were offerings to the god of the French.

Joliet asked these Indians for guides to the Wisconsin River. These were readily given. The Fox became narrower and narrower as it wound through marshes of wild rice; and, but for the guides, the Frenchmen would surely have lost their way.

Finally they reached a place where the Fox and Wisconsin rivers are only a mile and a half apart. They carried their canoes across this distance and launched them on the Wisconsin. They sailed down this peaceful river, among islands covered with trees and tangled grapevines until, on June 17th, they saw before them a mighty water which met the Wisconsin. They knew at once that it was the "Father of Waters," the Mississippi.

As the canoes floated easily down the great river there was no sign of human life anywhere.

One day they found human footprints in the mud on the western bank, and a path leading off into the prairies. Joliet and Marquette left the canoes with their men and started out upon the path.

After walking six miles they saw an Indian village a little way off. They stopped and prayed God to help them, and then went on until they could hear the voices of the Indians. Here they stood still and shouted. This caused great excitement in the village, and all the inhabitants turned out. Four of the warriors came forward with great dignity, holding up two calumets or peace pipes. Standing in front of the Frenchmen they looked at them in silence. When Marquette saw that they wore French cloth, he made up his mind that they were friends.

You may judge how glad he was when he found that these Indians were Illinois, members of the very tribe that had first told him of the great river, and that had often invited him to come and teach them.

After the peace pipes had been smoked, they went together to the village. The chief met them at the door of a large wigwam. He held up both hands to his eyes as if to shield them from a great light. "Frenchmen, how bright the sun shines when you come to visit us," he said. "Enter our wigwam in peace."

After once more smoking the peace pipe Marquette and Joliet were invited to go to another village to visit the great chief of all the Illinois.

Here Marquette spoke to the Indians in the Algonquin language and told them that he was a messenger of God to them. He told them also of Count Frontenac, the great Governor of Canada, and asked about the Mississippi and the tribes along its banks.

Then a great feast was served. After the feast was over buffalo robes were spread on the ground; and here Joliet and Marquette slept till morning, when the chief and six hundred of his men took them back to their canoes and bade them farewell as they went on their way.

Marquette and Joliet Floating Down the Mississippi

Down the great river they paddled, past the mouth of the Illinois and past the wonderful rocks which at this

Marquette Attacked by the Arkansas Indians

point line the eastern shore. On one of the rocks were painted two monsters. These were Indian gods. The voyagers were so excited over the strange picture that they scarcely noticed where they were going. Suddenly they saw before them a great torrent of yellow mud rushing out into the peaceful blue water and sweeping along on its current branches and uprooted trees. The canoes were whirled like chips upon the angry waters. They had reached the mouth of the Missouri. In spite of the danger, the travelers got safely past.

In a few days more they reached the mouth of the river which the Indians called the Ohio, or "Beautiful River." After they had passed this, the weather grew warmer very rapidly, and the mosquitoes tormented them day and night.

As Joliet and Marquette neared the mouth of the Arkansas River, they saw a group of wigwams on the western bank. The inhabitants stood waving their hatchets and yelling the war whoop. Boat loads of them came out on both sides of the white men, so that they

The Burial of Marquette

could go neither forward nor backward, while a swarm of daring young braves waded out into the river. The white men were terribly frightened and called upon the saints to protect them, Marquette holding up his peace pipe all the while. The young warriors paid no attention to this; but when the older ones saw it, they quieted the young braves and told the Frenchmen to come on shore. This they did, and were treated kindly.

Soon after this Marquette and Joliet began to consider what they should do next. They had gone far enough to make sure that the Mississippi flowed, not into the Gulf of California, but into the Gulf of Mexico. If they went on to the mouth of the river they might be killed by savage Indians, or by Spaniards. So they decided to go back to Canada and report what they had found.

The homeward journey through the July heat was very trying; and Father Marquette, who was never very strong, fell sick on the way. When the travelers came to the Illinois River they entered its mouth and made their way up its quiet waters, between shady forests, and grassy plains abounding in deer and buffalo. From one of the Indian villages along the shore, a young chief and his warriors acted as guides to Lake Michigan. Coasting along the edge of this lake, the party once more reached Green Bay. It was now the end of September. The travelers had been gone four months and had made a canoe voyage of more than two thousand five hundred miles.

Joliet went on to Quebec to tell Count Frontenac of all they had discovered. But Marquette was worn out by the hardships of the journey and stayed at Green Bay to rest.

The next fall he went to the home of the Illinois Indians. Here he preached to the savages until he felt that he was dying. Then he asked his companions to take him back to Green Bay.

But he did not live to reach Green Bay. His companions cared for him tenderly to the last and buried him on the shore of Lake Michigan.

XVIII

LA SALLE

His Plans and Early Explorations

WHEN Joliet reached Montreal with the news of his great discovery, he found there a very brave and strong-minded man named La Salle. And La Salle, hearing Joliet's story, asked Count Frontenac to let him go to France to tell the King of all that he had heard.

Frontenac gladly gave his permission, and in the year 1677 La Salle sailed for France. He told the King of the journey of Joliet and Marquette, of the fertile soil of the Mississippi valley, and the abundant game and the pleasant climate. He told him of the wool of the buffaloes, which could be used in making cloth, and of the hemp and cotton that grew wild along the banks of the great river.

"Now," said La Salle, "why should not all this rich land belong to France, instead of waiting for the English and Spanish to come and take it away from us before our very eyes?"

The King was pleased with what La Salle said, and gave him permission to make a voyage of discovery which should last not more than five years. He was to build forts wherever he thought it necessary.

In 1678 La Salle came back to Canada to prepare for his voyage through the west. He thought that, if he could start with a ship above the falls in the Niagara River, he would be able to sail up the river to the lakes, and then through the lakes to the Mississippi. He did not know that part of this distance lay overland.

Robert Cavalier de La Salle

So with his men he sailed up the Niagara as far as the falls. Then with their baggage on their backs the men plodded twelve miles through the forest until they reached a creek above the falls.

Here La Salle immediately set the men to work building a ship. He drove the first nail himself. When the work was well under way, he started back to Fort Frontenac on foot—a distance of two hundred and fifty miles through a snow-covered forest, with no food but roasted corn. This was in February, 1679.

It was summer before he returned to the Niagara. He found the ship all finished and towed out into the river. She had been named the *Griffon*.

In August, 1679, the voyagers left the Niagara River

and sailed out into Lake Erie. Through Lake Erie, Lake St. Clair, Lake Huron they went, and westward into Lake Michigan. At the entrance of Green Bay La Salle cast anchor.

Here he found some men whom he had sent ahead to buy furs of the Indians. He told these men to load the furs upon the *Griffon* and take them back to Niagara, where they would find men to carry them to Montreal. Then they were to come back again with the ship. So on a September morning the *Griffon* fired a parting shot and set sail for Niagara.

The Building of the "Griffon"

La Salle, with fourteen men and four canoes, went down the lake to the St. Joseph River. Here he built a fort and waited till December, hoping for the return of the *Griffon*; but no *Griffon* came. Finally he sent two men back to seek her while he with the others made his way up the St. Joseph River, until they came to the portage, or path, which led to the headwaters of the Illinois River.

191

Bronze Sun-Dial and Compass

Found in January, 1902, on the shores of Green Bay. Undoubtedly of the seventeenth century, and probably lost by some French fur trader or missionary.

As La Salle sailed down this river he came to an Indian encampment. He told the Indians that he had come to protect them against their enemies and to teach them about the true God. He told them also that he was going to build a great wooden canoe, with which to sail the Mississippi. This pleased the Indians, and they feasted and entertained the white men.

During the night some Indians, sent by the enemies of La Salle, came to the camp. These Indians told the Illinois that La Salle was going down the Mississippi to stir up the Arkansas tribes to fight against the Illinois. Then they crept stealthily away.

When morning came it was easy to tell that a change had come over the Illinois. After breakfast they began to talk about the terrible dangers of the river.

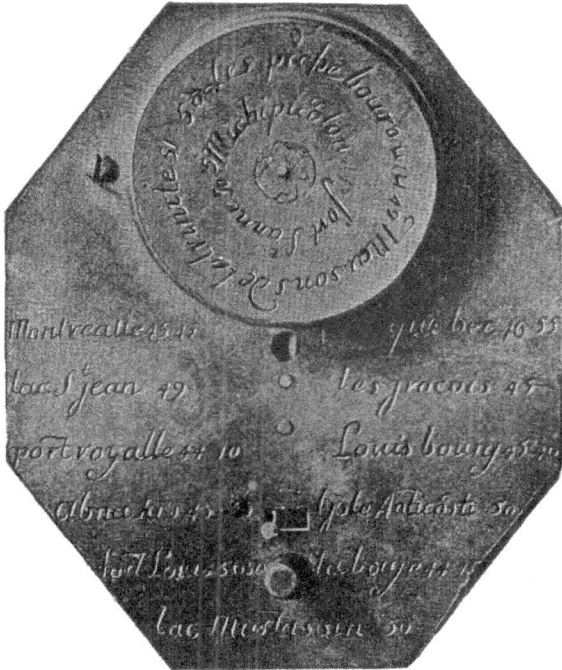

Reverse Side of Sun-Dial and Compass

Here are noted the names and latitudes of the principal French forts in the region of the St. Lawrence River.

"There are fierce monsters," they said, "which will devour white men. There are great whirlpools which will swallow your big canoe."

La Salle saw at once that his enemies had been at work. So he told the Indians that he was not afraid of monsters or whirlpools and that he was going on to the great river. But his men were of a different temper. Most of them were much alarmed by what they had heard. That night six of them ran away, and some others tried to poison their brave leader.

La Salle now went farther down the river, where he built a strong fort, which he called Crèvecoeur. This word means "Broken Heart." Surely La Salle had already had trouble enough to break any man's heart. His ship was lost, many of his men were unfaithful, his enemies in Canada were plotting against him.

And yet La Salle did not lose hope. Since his ship was gone, he resolved to build another. As the timber sawyers were among the men who had run away, La Salle said that he would saw the timbers himself, if one man would help him. This made the rest ashamed, and they all set to work.

In six weeks the ship was half done. But there were no anchors or cables or rigging. There was nothing to be done but to go back for these things to Fort Frontenac, a distance of one thousand miles. La Salle was not a man to hesitate at a little journey like this; so one day in March, with two canoes, an Indian hunter, and four Frenchmen, he started up the river.

It was a fearful journey. Sometimes pushing the canoes through the drifting ice, sometimes walking overland for many miles and carrying the canoes on their shoulders, sometimes in danger from the Iroquois, sometimes torn by brush and briers through which they made their way, the men kept bravely on until they reached the Niagara. By this time all but La Salle were worn out, so he left his companions at Niagara and took three fresh men in their stead.

It was May when he saw before him the walls of Fort Frontenac. Here he heard nothing but bad news. Not only was the *Griffon* lost, but a ship from France laden with La Salle's goods had been wrecked.

Still the brave leader did not give up. He went to Montreal for the supplies he wanted and returned with them to Fort Frontenac.

La Salle Reaches the Gulf of Mexico

IT would be a long story to tell of the adventures which befell La Salle before he again reached Fort Crèvecoeur. He did reach it, however, the following winter. Here he found his men were gone and his fort pulled to pieces, but the ship was almost as he had left it. On one of the planks was written in French the words, "We are all savages."

From Fort Crèvecoeur, La Salle and his companions pushed on down to the Mississippi, the great river which they had never before seen. Then turning his canoe, La Salle sailed back the way he had come.

In December, 1681, La Salle started once more on his dangerous journey. With him were twenty-three Frenchmen, besides about thirty Indians. They set out in their canoes from Fort Miami, on Lake Michigan, and entered the Chicago River. Finding it frozen, they made sledges and loaded the canoes and baggage on them. Then they crossed overland to the Illinois, and finally reached the Mississippi. At first the river was full of floating ice, but as they went farther south it became clear.

They sailed on past the place where the mighty Missouri empties its muddy stream into the Father of Waters, and past the mouth of the Ohio. Winter gave way to spring, the air became soft and warm, and the banks were bright with the fresh green of the unfolding leaves.

Louis XIV of France

Near the mouth of the Arkansas River La Salle raised a cross bearing the arms of France and took formal possession of the country for the French King. Then he went on south.

On the 6th of April La Salle found the river dividing into three streams. He separated his men into three parties, himself taking the western channel. As he drifted down the muddy stream, the salt smell of the sea reached him. The banks of the river disappeared. He had reached the Gulf of Mexico, his journey's end.

The three parties soon met. They landed upon a

piece of dry ground, a little way from the river's mouth. Here La Salle made a column, bearing the arms of France and these words, in French: "Louis the Great, King of France and of Navarre, rules here. April 9, 1682."

The Frenchmen were drawn up in martial array and sang hymns. Then, amid volleys of musketry and shouts of "Long live the King!" La Salle set up the column. He proclaimed in a loud voice that he was taking for France all the land extending from the head of the Ohio River to the mouth of the Mississippi, including all the rivers which flow into the Mississippi. To this vast region he gave the name of "Louisiana," or "Louis's land." It extended from the Alleghanies to the Rocky Mountains, and from the Gulf of Mexico to Canada.

La Salle's Attempted Settlement

In the year 1684 La Salle was in France for the last time. His purpose was to ask the King for one ship and two hundred men, that he might build a fort on the Mississippi. He would form an army of fifteen thousand Indians, he said, with which he could easily capture the Spanish silver mines. The King granted this request most generously. Instead of one ship he gave four, and recruiting agents were sent out to enlist the soldiers asked for.

La Salle's plan was to reach the mouth of the Mississippi River by crossing the Gulf of Mexico.

It was December before the little fleet entered the Gulf. On New Year's Day, 1685, they anchored about nine miles from the land. La Salle went ashore, but could find nothing that looked familiar. He had passed the mouth of the Mississippi without knowing it, and his great journey had been taken in vain.

Finally he entered Matagorda Bay on the coast of Texas, which he thought was the western mouth of the Mississippi. He ordered the ships to be brought within the bay, and the men to go ashore. The bay was shallow, and one of the ships was wrecked upon a reef. After building some houses for his little colony, La Salle started northward with about fifty of his men. They were gone five months and returned ragged and wearied, all but La Salle discouraged.

La Salle's fortunes were now in a very sad state. He had sent two of his ships back to France; and, a few days after his return, news came of the wreck of the one that he had kept. Many of the colony had died of disease, and La Salle himself was much broken in health. He resolved that he would find the Mississippi, journey to Canada, and get supplies for his colony. This was his last hope.

Everyone set to work to prepare for the journey. The sails of the wrecked vessels were cut up and pieced with deerskins to make coats for the men. On the 7th of January, 1687, La Salle made a farewell address to those who were to stay behind and with his men left the fort for the last time.

Across prairies and rivers they journeyed. In March they were still on the plains of northern Texas. One day the men fell into a quarrel about some buffalo meat. Three were killed, among them La Salle's nephew. La Salle, who knew nothing of this, asked one of the party where his nephew was. "He is skulking about somewhere," answered the man impudently.

La Salle rebuked him for his manner of speaking, when a shot whizzed from the grass, and the great leader fell dead. He had escaped the fury of flood and Indians, to die at the hands of one of his own countrymen; and the helpless colony in Texas was left to the mercy of the Spaniards.

XIX

LORD BALTIMORE

BESIDES the faith of Pilgrims and Puritans there was yet another creed in England—that of the Roman Catholics. Like the Puritans, the Catholics were not allowed to live in peace and worship God according to their conscience. So they, too, wanted to move to America and start life anew.

George Calvert, Lord Baltimore, felt that the Catholics were right in their desire; and he resolved to become their leader and help them all he could toward establishing their new colony. The English King granted Lord Baltimore plenty of land in Newfoundland; and there, in 1623, he sent his colonists.

Whether these colonists were long-suffering and uncomplaining, or whether their complaints were unheeded, it is hard to say. Be that as it may, for four years they lived in Newfoundland and no one bothered about them. At the end of that time, Lord Baltimore and his family left England to make their home in the Newfoundland colony. They expected to find a paradise; but what they found was very different.

Before long, Lord Baltimore was writing the

King that the land was not at all what he had believed it to be; that the hard winters lasted from the middle of October to the middle of May; and that both the land and the water was so frozen up all those months that proper food was out of the question. Possibly Newfoundland was a splendid country for

George Calvert,
the First Lord Baltimore

fishermen and those used to storms and tempests, but surely it was no place for Lord Baltimore's Catholic colony. That nobleman now wanted to take his people to Virginia, and he desired the King to grant him land in that warmer region.

Then, without waiting for the King's answer, Lord Baltimore sailed with his family and some others to visit Virginia. He was going to be sure this time what his colonists would have to expect.

In October, 1629, Lord Baltimore reached Jamestown. The welcome he received was hardly what he had hoped for. The Virginians were suspicious of him and took no pains to hide their feelings. Why should he come to their part of the land? They did not want him and his followers. In spite of them, however, Lord Baltimore stayed long enough to look over the country and to decide that it suited him in every way.

This settled, he went back to England and petitioned Charles I to grant him a strip of land north of the Potomac River, which was not inhabited by English. King Charles consented, and a charter was drawn up. But before it was completed, Lord Baltimore died.

Fortunately Lord Baltimore had a son who was as eager as his father to find a home for his Catholic friends. And it was this son, the second Lord Baltimore, who founded and guided the new English colony during its first years in its new lands.

The old Lord Baltimore's charter was given to the second Lord Baltimore, Cecil Calvert. Leonard Calvert, the second son, was appointed governor of the new colony; and in November, 1633, he sailed with about three hundred people for America.

Early in 1634 the colonists entered Chesapeake Bay and sailed to the mouth of the Potomac. Here they found the country all their hearts could wish for. On the northern bank of the Potomac not far from its mouth lay an Indian village. The settlers were charmed with the spot and were very anxious to make their home there. Governor Calvert therefore bought the village from the Indians, giving for it some hatchets, hoes, and cloth; and the English landed as rightful possessors.

The new colony received the name of Maryland in honor of Henrietta Maria, the English Queen. And the ready-made town was called St. Mary's.

Unlike the Puritans and the Virginians, the

*Governor Calvert, Bartering for Land
on Chesapeake Bay*

From the center panel of C. Y. Turner's mural
painting in the new Baltimore Court House.

Maryland settlers did not have to till an uncultivated ground. The Indians from whom they had bought the land had enriched the soil, laid out fields, and planted corn and other grains. The great forests, too, were full of game; and the best of fish were to be had for the catching. Good fortune smiled on the newcomers.

Such a prosperous beginning promised much for the future. New settlers soon followed on the heels of the first arrivals, and the little town of St. Mary's was quickly surrounded by tidy, well-kept farms.

There were many things to draw settlers to Maryland. But perhaps the greatest attraction was that the new colony offered a home to any Christian whether Catholic or Protestant. Although founded as a refuge for Catholics, Lord Baltimore did not want his colony to close its doors on anyone who was suffering for religious views. All were welcomed to Maryland.

At first it seemed as if this good man's best hopes for his colony might be fulfilled. The settlers were on friendly terms with the Indians. They had no fear of starvation, and their country became a recognized retreat for Puritans and others who wished to have freedom in religion.

But when the Virginia colonists heard that Charles had granted Lord Baltimore the tract of land known as Maryland, they remonstrated and petitioned him to retract his grant. They said the land belonged to them by right of their first charter. However, the King refused to listen to them and allowed Lord Baltimore and his people to retain their charter.

Now, though the King had settled the question to his own satisfaction, his decision by no means pleased the Virginians. They regarded the Catholics with an evil eye and determined to create trouble for them. Chief among the creators of this trouble was a man by the name of William Clayborne, a member of the Jamestown council.

Before the Maryland settlers came to America, Clayborne had obtained from the King the right to trade in the region around the Potomac and, in fact, in any part of North America not controlled by some monopoly; and he had established a fur-trading settlement on the Isle of Kent.

The island of Kent was included in the land granted to Lord Baltimore, and one of Governor Calvert's first acts on reaching America was to see Clayborne. Treating him with all tenderness, the new governor still impressed it upon the fur trader that the island of

Kent belonged to Maryland, and to Maryland alone. He might colonize it and welcome, but he must not forget that he was settling on Lord Baltimore's land.

Clayborne laid the matter before the Virginia council. They said that Governor Calvert was all wrong, and that the island of Kent belonged to Virginia. So this little island became a bone of contention.

Clayborne made the first move. He tried to arouse the Indians against the new colonists by saying that they were hated Spaniards.

Next the Maryland settlers seized one of Clayborne's trading ships and sold it with all its cargo. For this Clayborne sent out an armed sloop to make raids on Maryland's shipping. Then Governor Calvert sent two armed ships after Clayborne's one and captured it. Six men were killed.

A few days later, there was another battle and more bloodshed. This time Clayborne was victorious, and for over two years he held undisturbed possession of the island of Kent.

In 1637 Clayborne's London partners in the fur trade became dissatisfied with the number of furs they were receiving. So they sent a new man to look after the island of Kent, and ordered Clayborne to come to England. With Clayborne once out of the way, the new man in charge of the island of Kent turned it over to Governor Calvert. And the Maryland governor took not only the island, but all of Clayborne's property that he could lay his hands on. Clayborne tried to find some hope of redress in London, but could not. So he came back to Virginia and patiently awaited his turn.

After a few years it came. Clayborne and a man named Ingle combined in an attack upon Maryland. Clayborne recovered his island of Kent, and Ingle captured the town of St. Mary's. Governor Calvert was obliged to flee to Virginia. Two years later he came back at the head of a small army and once more drove out the intruders.

But this was not the end. In 1649 King Charles I was beheaded. A new government was set up. And in 1652 this new government sent a body of commissioners to inspect "the colonies within the Bay of Chesapeake." One of the commissioners was Clayborne. Here was his chance for a last word. The Governor of Maryland was removed from office,

Charles I of England

a new governor was elected, and Lord Baltimore was declared to have no right in the colony.

You can imagine with what grief Lord Baltimore saw all this strife going on. He had tried all these years to have his colonists keep peace with the Indians and their English neighbors. And he had endeavored to found a settlement broad in views and generous in religious beliefs. Was all this noble effort to be destroyed by a few men who did not seem to have any conscience at all? About four years later Maryland was restored to Lord Baltimore; and the colony, its troubles over, once more grew and prospered.

When Cecil Calvert died, his eldest son succeeded him as proprietor of Maryland.

During the years Lord Baltimore had governed Maryland, the colonists had learned to love and respect him. He had been a kind father to his people and had done everything possible for their welfare. On his death the colonists sincerely mourned him and never forgot his many good qualities and unselfish acts.

XX

WILLIAM PENN

The Quakers

WHILE everyone in England was quarreling about the right way to worship God, a weaver's son, tending his master's sheep and reading his Bible, found what he thought was the true way. Through his study of the Bible, and through prayer, he came to believe that God had sent His Son into the world that men might learn to live at peace and to love one another.

This man was George Fox, the founder of the Society of Friends, or Quakers, as they came to be called. He went about preaching; and everywhere many people believed in what he said and joined the Society, although they were again and again thrown into prison for believing and preaching this strange new religion of peace and brotherhood.

The Quakers had many beliefs and customs that seemed strange and wrong to the people of other churches. They believed that all men were equal in the sight of God; and so they would not take off their hats to show honor to any man, not even the King.

They addressed everyone as "thee" and "thou," because the pronoun "you" was then used to express respect to a superior. They said that if "thee" and "thou" were good enough for God, they were surely good enough for men.

They thought that no man should take pay for preaching the Gospel, and so they refused to pay taxes to support the English Church.

They did not believe in witchcraft, though at that time men and women were being burned as witches in both England and America.

They believed that women should have equal rights with men.

They believed that the teachings of the Bible should be obeyed; and as the Good Book says "Swear not at all," they would not even take the oath of allegiance to the King.

And since the Bible says, "Blessed are the peacemakers," they would not quarrel with anyone, or seek revenge, or bear arms, even in defense of their own country.

Yet they were a brave people. They would go anywhere and speak what they believed to be true and right, though they knew that they would be cast into prison for it.

I must tell you how they came to be called Quakers. Once their founder, George Fox, was taken before a judge and accused of breaking the law, because he had been preaching in the streets. He bade the judge to "tremble before the Lord." Since "quake" and "tremble" have the same meaning, the Society of Friends came to be called Quakers from this incident. The Quakers approved of dressing very plainly. "If people think too much of their clothes," they said, "they will become proud and envious." They loved to remember that Abraham and Isaac were herdsmen, that John the Baptist wore a rough garment of camel's hair, and, greatest of all, that the Savior was born in a manger and was brought up in a carpenter's home and chose poor workingmen for His followers and friends.

In the year 1660 there was at the University of Oxford a strong, handsome young man by the name of William Penn. One day a Quaker preacher came to Oxford. Penn and many of the other students heard him and were convinced that he spoke the truth. From this time on, Penn refused to wear the student's gown, because, he said, it showed pride. He and some of the other students began to hold Quaker meetings. For this they were expelled from the University.

William Penn's father was an admiral in the British navy and had no use for the peaceful ways of the Quakers. When his son came home Admiral Penn was very angry. He tried to make William say that he would no longer be a Quaker. But William would not yield. His father even whipped him, but it did no good. Finally he was turned out of doors.

William's mother was a very wise and lovely woman and soon persuaded her husband to let their son come home again. Admiral Penn now decided to send the young man traveling, in order that he might forget the Quakers. So he sent him through Europe, and for several years the young man traveled, learning foreign languages and seeing the greatest cities of the world.

But he did not forget the Quakers. When he was twenty-two years of age he was in Ireland looking after some business for his father. Here he heard the same preacher whom he had heard at Oxford. In the same year William Penn was put in jail for being one of a crowd of people who listened to Quaker preaching. When he was set free his father sent for him to come home immediately. He told him that he must give up the ways of the Quakers. William said that he could not do this. Finally Admiral Penn said that if William would take off his hat before King Charles II, the Duke of York, and himself, he should be forgiven everything else. But William said that he could not do even this. So he was once more turned out of his father's house.

Fortunately Mrs. Penn helped her son with money, so that he did not suffer. The King and the Duke of York, too, were always friendly to him for his father's sake.

Once when William went to see King Charles, the King took off his hat.

"Friend Charles," said Penn, "why dost thou remove thy hat?"

"Because," said the King, "where I am, it is the custom for only one to remain covered."

William Penn was put in prison many times for writing about and preaching the Quaker religion.

Penn's father soon saw that his son was determined to remain a Quaker, and a very true one. So once more he permitted him to come home and never again interfered with his religious belief.

When the old admiral was dying, he sent to his friend, the Duke of York, and asked that he and his brother, King Charles II, would be friends to William. Both promised and kept their word.

The Settlement of Pennsylvania

THE Quakers, persecuted everywhere, looked longingly toward America as a place where they might live in peace and do God's will as they saw it. A few had gone to Massachusetts, where they had been treated very badly by the Puritans. Some had gone to Rhode Island, and had received a hearty welcome. Several settlements had been made in East Jersey, while in West Jersey a colony of about four hundred Quakers had been planted.

Now King Charles owed William Penn's father a debt of sixteen thousand pounds. As the King knew how to make debts a great deal better than how to pay them, the debt was still unpaid when Admiral Penn died.

The First Settlements of Pennsylvania and New Jersey

In 1680 William Penn went to the King and asked him for a tract of land in America. The idea pleased Charles very much. It was far easier to give away a piece of woodland which he had never seen and knew nothing about than it would have been to raise the money to pay the debt. So he gave Penn a charter, granting him a tract of land north of Maryland and bounded on the east by the Delaware River. Penn was given the right to make and execute laws, to appoint judges, receive settlers, establish a military force, make cities, and carry on foreign trade.

Penn wanted to call his province New Wales, because Wales is a very mountainous country, and Penn had heard that there were mountains beyond the Delaware River. But King Charles did not like this name, so Penn called it "Sylvania," which is a Latin name meaning "woodland." The King added "Penn" to this name, making it "Pennsylvania." William did not approve of this, for he thought that it looked like vanity; but Charles laughed and said, "We are not naming the province to honor you, but to honor the Admiral, your noble father." So Penn had to be content.

Before long Penn had sent to his province twenty ships with about three thousand people, most of them Quakers. In 1682 he came himself, leaving his wife and children in England. Late in October he landed at Newcastle, on Delaware Bay, where the Dutch and Swedish settlers welcomed him with shouts of joy.

The same day, Penn sailed on up the river until he came to Chester, where some of his settlers had already built their homes. Here he called an assembly of the people to make the laws for their colony. Everyone took part in the assembly. The people of Delaware wanted to join Penn's government and were received at once. The assembly made the following laws:

1. Everyone should be allowed to worship God according to his own conscience.

2. The first day of the week was to be kept as a day of rest.

3. All the members of the family were to be considered equal in the sight of the law.

4. No oath was to be required in any court of justice.

5. Everyone who paid his taxes was to have the right of voting.

6. Every Christian should have the right to hold office.

7. No tax could be collected except by law.

8. There were to be no bullfights, or cockfights, or stage-plays.

9. Murder was to be the only crime punishable by death.

10. Every prison was to be made a workhouse, where the prisoners should be taught how to do useful things and live a better life.

After these laws were made Penn set out to select a site for the city which he had planned before sailing from England. He chose a neck of land between the Schuylkill

The FRAME of the
GOVERNMENT
OF THE
Province of Pennsilvania
IN
AMERICA:
Together with certain
L A W S
Agreed upon in England
BY THE
GOVERNOUR
AND
Divers FREE-MEN of the aforesaid.
PROVINCE

To be further Explained and Confirmed there by the first *Provincial Council* and *General Assembly* that shall be held, if they see meet.

Printed in the Year MDCLXXXII.

Facsimile of the Title Page of Penn's Code of Laws

and Delaware rivers. Here he laid out Philadelphia, the city of freedom. "Philadelphia" is a Greek word, which means "brotherly love"; and Penn meant that brotherly love should rule his city.

The city was laid out like a checkerboard, with broad streets and large lots. Each house was to be built in the center of a lot, so that there might be large and beautiful lawns and also as little danger from fire as possible.

The streets were named after different kinds of trees.

Penn called a meeting of the Indians. They came armed and painted, but Penn and his friends were unarmed and plainly dressed, with the exception that Penn wore a sky-blue sash. He told the Indians that the Quakers had come to be their friends, and that they never carried arms.

Then he read a treaty of peace for the Indians and the Quakers, which the Indians gladly agreed to. The white men were to buy all land of the Indians, not to take it by force. If there was a dispute between white men and Indians, it was to be settled by a council of six white men and six Indians.

After the treaty was agreed to, Penn gave the Indians some presents and then walked with them, sat on the ground with them, and ate with them of roasted acorns and hominy. The Indians were very much pleased with this and began to hop and jump to show their delight. Thereupon Penn sprang to his feet and outdanced them all.

The Indians kept the treaty for many years, living

in peace and friendship with the Quakers.

Penn Reading the Treaty to the Indians

The "City of Brotherly Love" grew rapidly. By the end of 1683 there were three hundred and fifty-seven houses, many built of frame, many of bright-red brick, and still others of logs. By 1685 Philadelphia was a thriving town of twenty-five hundred people.

But William Penn did not have much opportunity to enjoy his colony. In 1684 he received word that the Quakers in England were again being cruelly persecuted. So he sailed for England, hoping soon to be able to return to Pennsylvania. However, it was fifteen years before Penn once more sailed for America, years full of deepest sorrow for him. His enemies in England had made a great deal of trouble for him; and, saddest of all, death had robbed him of his noble wife and several of his children. When he did return to Pennsylvania in 1699, he found Philadelphia a city of seven hundred houses and four thousand people.

House in Philadelphia in Which Penn Lived, 1699-1701

Penn stayed in America for two years, part of the time living in Philadelphia, and part of the time in a beautiful country home. Sometimes he would ride to and from the city on horseback, and sometimes he would sail on the Delaware in a little six-oared boat.

One day the Governor of New Jersey met him in his boat, struggling against wind and tide.

"I am surprised," said the Governor, "that you venture out against such a wind and tide."

"I have been struggling against wind and tide all my life," replied Penn.

In 1701 his business called him back to England, and he never had an opportunity to return to America.

But the colony planted in brotherly love lived and prospered. To-day Pennsylvania is one of the greatest of the States of the Union, and Philadelphia is one of the most beautiful cities.

XXI

GENERAL JAMES OGLETHORPE

It is a sad experience to get a necessity and then find it utterly impossible to raise the money to pay for it. This means debt, and debt often means suffering to honest men.

And if debt means suffering here in America to-day, picture what it must have meant in England in the eighteenth century, when to owe money was held a serious crime. The English laws were very strict. Let a man owe even a very small amount, and absolute ruin stared him in the face. No matter if his poverty came from sickness or misfortune. No matter if he had a large family to care for. If he could not pay his bills, an officer appeared and dragged him off to prison. There he could not earn a cent to pay his debt, and yet there he must stay. If his friends brought him food and comforts, all well and good; otherwise he might starve. His great hope of freedom was that his creditor would withdraw his claim, and this was often a very slight hope.

Now, the debtors' prisons were often visited by an English general, James Oglethorpe. He was of a kind and sympathetic nature, and it seemed to him a dreadful thing—this imprisonment for debt. Was there no way to help these poor people in their misery?

While he was pondering as to what he could do, an opportunity came. The English colony of South Carolina in America lay exposed to attacks from the Spaniards in Florida. The South Carolina settlers needed protection on the south. Here was Oglethorpe's chance. Why could not the most deserving of the poor imprisoned debtors be taken to America? And why could they not be settled in a colony which would serve as a military outpost against the Spaniards?

George III of England

General Oglethorpe laid his scheme before the English King and the English Government. Both heartily approved. The land lying between the Savannah and the Altamaha rivers was granted to the new colony. The colony was named Georgia in honor of King George III, and General Oglethorpe was appointed governor.

In January, 1733, General Oglethorpe, his released debtors and their families, entered the Savannah River. Upon the arrival of the settlers, an Indian chief came forward and welcomed them. "Here is a present for you," said he to Oglethorpe. It was a buffalo hide, painted on the inside with the head and feathers of an eagle. "The feathers are soft and signify love, the buffalo skin is the emblem of protection; therefore love and protect us and our families," said the chief. From this time the Indians were kindly treated by Oglethorpe; and, as usual, they rewarded friendship with friendship.

James Oglethorpe

The settlers bought from the Indians the land along the southern bank of the Savannah River, laid out a town, and named it Savannah.

Later other emigrants came and made other settlements in Georgia. These were persecuted Protestants from Germany and Austria, Scotch peasants from the Highlands, and even a small party of settlers from New England.

True to his promise to make his colony a military outpost against the Spaniards, Governor Oglethorpe built forts and insisted on military drills.

There were other things he insisted upon. No liquor could be imported into the colony, and no colonist could have slaves. Having no slaves, the settlers themselves were forced to work. The raising of rice and indigo were the chief occupations.

Before many years General Oglethorpe had a chance to prove that his colony made a valuable protection for South Carolina. In 1739 war broke out between Spain and England. The next spring Oglethorpe gathered an army of colonists and friendly Indians and marched into Florida. For five weeks the English besieged St. Augustine. Then they had to retreat.

The Spaniards now determined to invade Georgia. Great preparations were made. Finally thirty-six vessels with a large army sailed northward and landed on St. Simon's Island. Although Oglethorpe's force was nowhere near so great as the Spanish, he defeated them through strategy. The Spaniards fled to their vessels and never disturbed the English in Georgia again.

For ten years Governor Oglethorpe devoted himself to his colony. In 1743 he bade adieu to his sorrowing friends, both the settlers and the Indians, and left for his English home. Here he lived to a good old age, honored and loved by his countrymen as much as by the unfortunate debtors whom he had treated so kindly.

XXII

NATHANIEL BACON

In the year 1660 Sir William Berkeley was proclaimed Governor of Virginia under King Charles II of England, son of the beheaded Charles I.

The settlers must have had mixed feelings about Sir William's becoming governor. He was no stranger to them. He had been their governor once before.

During his first term, William Berkeley had proved himself a man of very decided ideas. His mind once made up, was made up for good and all. Moreover, he had been extremely loyal to the English king. What the King had wanted the colonists to do, Governor Berkeley had wanted them to do. And it made no difference whether the settlers themselves liked it or not. He placed little value on the colonists' own ideas of how their colony should be run. He did not believe in free schools, where all the children could be educated. He thought that education should be only for people with money and power. And yet, in spite of all this, the colony had done well under Governor Berkeley, and in many ways the settlers had approved of him.

The years that Sir William had been out of office do

not seem to have improved him. On becoming governor again, he still had all his old faults; and now he added some new ones. He was selfish and put his own good ahead of that of the colony: he liked to take his comfort undisturbed, and he was more set in his ways than ever. This was hard for the colonists to stand.

But worse was to come. The English king, Charles II, decreed that the tobacco raised in Virginia must be carried only to England and in English ships; and the colonists were forbidden to buy foreign goods unless they were handled by English merchants. The colonists protested that this would mean ruin to the colony's commerce. It made no difference. Moreover, heavy taxes for public improvements were imposed and enforced; but the improvements were never seen.

It is no wonder that between the tax collectors and their unsympathetic governor, the poor settlers began to grow bitter. No one seemed to be looking out for their interests.

Then still another grievance was added to the long list. Governor Berkeley refused to give the settlers protection against the Indians.

The raising of tobacco had had its effect on the colonial way of living. Large fields and many of them were needed, if large crops of tobacco were to be raised. The bigger the crops, the bigger the owner's returns. So instead of living in cozy little villages, the Virginia colonists laid out large farms or plantations, one beyond another, and thus spread their colony over a great territory. One's next-door neighbor lived a long way off, and it took some time to ride from home to home. This living far apart made it hard to guard against Indian attacks. While a plantation owner was trying to get help, his whole family might be killed.

From time to time the Indians had caused the Virginians more or less trouble. At last they saw that the English were quarreling among themselves over taxes and such matters. Here was a fine opportunity for the savages.

First, three settlers were killed on the Potomac. Then, growing bolder, the Indians crept down the James River and killed thirty-six Virginians.

Still Governor Berkeley took no steps to punish the murderers. He was afraid that, if he attacked the warriors, it might put an end to his profitable fur trade with their tribes. So the Indians went on plundering and killing the settlers and laying waste their homes. Before many months, they had killed large numbers of the colonists.

The people begged Governor Berkeley to help them, but he refused. "Very well, then, we will help ourselves," said Nathaniel Bacon.

This Nathaniel Bacon was a wealthy young planter who had lately brought his young wife to live in Virginia. He was tall, energetic, and commanding. He owned a plantation near where now the city of Richmond stands. One day in May, 1676, word was brought him that the Indians had attacked his plantation and killed the overseer and a servant. This was the last straw.

Bacon promptly called upon his neighbors to meet him. When they came, he reminded them that the Governor had failed to take any steps to avenge the lives of the slain colonists; that he was acting not for their good but for his own; and that something must be done at once to protect the Virginians from their deadly foes. He, Nathaniel Bacon, was ready to take matters into his own hands, he said. Were his neighbors not ready to do the same? If so, he begged them to choose a leader and to prepare to march against the warriors.

With a shout the colonists declared that Bacon was right. They would certainly have revenge for the death of their friends, and Bacon should lead them.

As a final effort at keeping terms with Governor Berkeley, Bacon sent to ask him for a commission. The Governor refused.

Then he would march without a commission. So the little army set out with Nathaniel Bacon at its head and marched up the James River. Finding the Indians in the forests, the colonists fell upon them and utterly routed them. This done they turned toward home.

While Bacon and his followers were fighting the Indians, Governor Berkeley was raging in Jamestown. Nathaniel Bacon was a rebel, he declared, and so were all the men in his party. Had they not marched contrary to his orders? Such men should be punished. For this purpose the Governor called out a body of troops and made ready to attack the rebels. He found, however, that Bacon had the sympathy of the colony back of him. So, fearing a general uprising, Sir William disbanded his troops and meekly gave in.

Now a new assembly was chosen, and Nathaniel Bacon was elected one of its members. When he arrived in Jamestown, he was seized and taken before the Governor, who was still very angry with him. A stormy interview followed. At last Bacon said that if the Governor would now give him a commission to fight the Indians, he would publicly admit that he had acted illegally in marching without one in the first place. It was agreed. Bacon admitted his faults. But the Governor still failed to give him the coveted commission.

Bacon Confronting the Governor in the Square

It was now Bacon's turn to be angry. He determined that he would have that commission. He left Jamestown, went home and collected another army of planters. With this army he marched back to Jamestown, drew up his forces in the public square, and sent word to Governor Berkeley that he was waiting for his commission.

Trembling with fury the Governor rushed out of the Statehouse and into the square, where he faced the men. There he threw back the ruffles of his shirt, bared his breast, and shouted, "Here I am! Shoot me! 'Fore God a fair mark, a fair mark—shoot!"

"No," Bacon calmly answered. "May it please your Honor, we have not come to hurt a hair of your head or of any man's. We have come for a commission to save our lives from the Indians, which you have so often promised; and now we will have it before we go." And Nathaniel Bacon was given his commission.

Once more he advanced on the warring tribes. By fall, these tribes were completely crushed, and the dreaded attacks on the plantations came to an end.

But Bacon did not have smooth sailing all this time. The Governor had again proclaimed Bacon and his followers rebels and had raised an army to defeat them. Bacon was not to be put down. He was doing his duty, and he would fight the Governor before he would give in. So he led his men against Governor Berkeley and his army.

On the march to Jamestown, Bacon stopped at the homes of those planters who had sided with the Governor, and, taking their wives prisoners, carried them along as hostages.

At Jamestown he found the Governor's troops ready for him. Placing the women in front of his own men he ordered an entrenchment dug and breastworks thrown up. While this was being done the Governor's guns did not fire a single shot for fear of killing the women.

The next day, however, there was a battle in Jamestown; and Bacon came off victor. The Governor fled from the town, boarded a ship, and sailed down the river.

With Jamestown once in his hands and the Governor gone, it would seem as if Bacon should have been satisfied; but he was not. He realized that even though he remained conqueror in Virginia, the King might send war ships and soldiers from England, and a great many unpleasant things might happen. So he decided first of all to burn the city of Jamestown.

The Ruins of Jamestown

It was on the 19th of September, 1676, that they set fire to the city; and in a few hours the whole town was reduced to ashes. Undoubtedly many a man and woman wept when they saw their homes eaten up by the flames. But they made no effort to prevent Bacon from doing as he thought right.

However, the "Bacon Rebellion," as it was called, was not to last much longer. The very next month after the burning of Jamestown, came the death from fever of the daring young Nathaniel Bacon. And with no leader, his army disbanded and went home. Then Governor Berkeley came back to Virginia ready for revenge, and he had it. More than twenty of the rebels were executed, and many more would have died had not the council decided that blood enough had been shed.

When King Charles II in England heard of Governor Berkeley's deeds of revenge, he said, "The old fool has taken away more lives in that naked country than I did for the murder of my father."

XXIII

BENJAMIN FRANKLIN

Boyhood

In the early part of the eighteenth century, when Boston was a little town of less than ten thousand inhabitants, there lived just opposite the Old South Church a good soap boiler and candle maker, named Josiah Franklin. He had seven daughters and ten sons. And this story is about the youngest of his sons, Benjamin, who was born in Boston, January 6, 1706.

With so many mouths to feed, Josiah Franklin could not afford to keep any one of his children long in school. However, Benjamin learned to read when he was very young, and at the age of eight he was sent to the Latin Grammar School. The next year he went to a school where arithmetic and writing were taught. These two years were all that he spent in school.

Like most boys who live near the sea, Benjamin Franklin was a good swimmer and could handle a boat like an old seaman. Like most boys, too, he was always on the lookout for adventure and sometimes led his friends into trouble.

One of his favorite playgrounds was on the edge of a salt marsh, where at high tide he could fish for minnows. Running about on its banks the boys had trampled them into a mere quagmire. The mud was so deep that the fun was spoiled. What could they do? Never at a loss for some way out of his difficulties, Benjamin was ready with a scheme. Not far from the marsh a new house was being built, and the builders had already brought the stones and piled them ready for use. Why couldn't the boys get these stones and build a wharf in the mud? The very thing, they all thought.

The Birthplace of Franklin

So that night after the workmen had left the new house, Benjamin and his friends met there and began to move the stones. Some of them were pretty large and very heavy, and it took two or three boys to carry them. But they worked as hard and fast as they could, until they got all the stones to the edge of the marsh and their wharf built.

Picture the surprised workmen when they went to use their stones in the morning! Not one was left. Who could have taken them and where were they? A search was made. The little wharf was soon discovered, and word was sent to the fathers of the boys.

Franklin says of the occasion, "Several of us were corrected by our fathers; and though I pleaded the usefulness of the work, mine convinced me that nothing was useful which was not honest."

In olden times boys began quite early to learn some trade. The natural thing for a boy to do was to learn his father's trade. So for two years after leaving school Benjamin worked for his father, cutting wicks, molding candles, tending shop, and running errands. As he did not like this kind of work in the least, Mr. Franklin took him to see bricklayers, joiners, tanners, and cutters at their work. Not one of these trades suited the boy.

At last, his great liking for the few books at his command persuaded his father to make a printer of him. Benjamin's brother James was a printer; and when the lad was twelve years old, he was apprenticed to this elder brother. In return for his board and clothes, and for being taught the printer's trade, Benjamin was to work for his brother until he was twenty-one.

Once in the printing house, Benjamin had better opportunities for reading. Often the booksellers would lend him books, which he would sit up all night to read that they might be returned in the morning. One of James Franklin's friends took a fancy to the boy and invited him to his own library, loaning him as many books as he cared to read.

Inspired by his reading he began to practice writing and worked at it faithfully, always trying to improve his language. All day long he worked hard at his trade; but in the early mornings, in the evenings, and on Sundays, he would read and write to his heart's content. It was through his ability in writing that Benjamin Franklin was able to do great good in later life, as you shall see.

A Printing Press of Franklin's Day

Two years after Benjamin went to work for his brother, James began to print a newspaper which he called the *New England Courant*. Benjamin was very anxious to write something for this paper, but he was sure that James would not print anything if he knew that it had been written by his little brother. So one night Benjamin slipped under the door of the printing house a little story that he had written. James Franklin found it and showed it to some of his friends. All agreed that it had been written by some very clever man. This delighted the young writer, and he kept up his secret writings for some time, enjoying the joke on James immensely.

When Benjamin was sixteen, James printed something in his paper which the Massachusetts Assembly did not like. They therefore refused to let him publish the *New England Courant* any more. So he decided to print the paper under the name of Benjamin Franklin.

Now the paper was more clever than ever before. Every number was full of fresh news and lively jokes. The paper sold like hot cakes. Things would have gone very well had not James Franklin proved a harsh master to his young brother, often beating him.

Finally Benjamin could bear it no longer and left the printing house. This made James very angry. He went around to all the other printers in Boston and told them not to give Benjamin any work. Surely this was a sorry plight for the young printer.

Early Life in Philadelphia

UNABLE to get work in Boston, young Franklin decided to slip away on a packet boat which was going to New York. This meant a sea journey of three hundred miles and was quite an undertaking for those days. In October, 1723, he reached New York, a lad of seventeen, an entire stranger in the city, with very little money in his pocket.

He went to William Bradford, the only printer in New York. Mr. Bradford had no work for him, but advised Benjamin to go to Philadelphia, a hundred miles farther south, where his son was a printer.

Franklin set out in a boat that was going to Amboy on the coast of New Jersey. The sea was rough, and the trip took thirty hours. As there was neither food nor water on the boat, he felt hungry and sick by the time Amboy was reached.

The next morning it was raining hard; but Franklin started on foot to Burlington, a distance of fifty miles. All day he walked. That night he stopped at a poor inn, soaking wet and very tired. He wished that he had never left home. Early the next morning he was on his way again; and when evening came, he found himself within ten miles of Burlington. On the third morning he reached Burlington, where he found a boat which was going to Philadelphia that evening.

As there was no wind, the whole distance had to be rowed. When midnight came, nothing had been seen of Philadelphia. Probably impressed by the amount of rowing they had done, some of the men insisted that they must have passed the city, and that they would go no farther. So there was nothing to do but to land and wait for the morning. A fire was built with the rails of an old fence, and the men huddled around it until dawn.

Then Philadelphia was seen a little way ahead; and by nine o'clock Franklin had left his traveling companions and was wandering alone up one of the streets of the Quaker city.

It is no wonder that after all his travel and lack of rest Franklin was tired and hungry. The first thing he did was to try to find out where he could get some breakfast. A boy directed him to a bakeshop. It seems that bread must have cost more in Boston than in Philadelphia; for when Franklin asked for a modest threepenny worth, to his surprise he was handed out three great puffy loaves. They were much too large to put into his pockets, so he tucked one under each arm and, eating the third, went on up the street.

As luck would have it, he sauntered thus by the house of a certain Mr. Read, just as little Miss Read was standing in the doorway. And this young lady, little dreaming that she was looking at her future husband, could not keep from laughing at the poor awkward young stranger.

Franklin's Arrival in Philadelphia

After finding a lodging house and being refreshed by a good night's rest, Franklin started out to find Bradford, the printer. Mr. Bradford did not need any help, so Franklin went to the only other printer in the city, a man by the name of Keimer; and here he was given work.

Keimer got Franklin a boarding place at Mr. Read's, the very house where the saucy young lady had laughed at him. Franklin says, "My chest and clothes being come by this time, I made rather a more respectable appearance in the eyes of Miss Read than I had done when she first happened to see me, eating my roll on the street."

While Franklin was working for Keimer, his brother-in-law, Captain Holmes, who was at Newcastle, wrote urging the young man to go home. When the captain received the answer, he showed it to the Governor of Pennsylvania, who happened to be with him. The Governor read the letter and was surprised that a boy of seventeen could write so well.

One day when Franklin and Keimer were at work near the window of the printing house, they saw two finely dressed gentlemen coming to the door. Keimer thought of course that the distinguished visitors were for him. He was very much surprised when one of them said that he was the Governor of Pennsylvania and wanted to see Benjamin Franklin.

The Governor told Benjamin that there was great need of a good printer in the colonies, and that if he would set up in business for himself he should have all the public printing of Pennsylvania and Delaware. This was indeed an honor.

Furthermore the Governor offered to send Franklin to London that he might choose for himself those things necessary for his start as an independent printer. Of course Franklin was delighted, and when the yearly ship sailed from Philadelphia to London he was one of its passengers. He was to find letters of credit from the Governor waiting for him on his ship, but for some unaccountable reason the Governor failed to send them. This fact Franklin did not discover until the ship had almost reached England. And soon he was alone in London, the greatest city in the world, without money or friends.

However, Benjamin Franklin was not to be easily discouraged. He soon found employment in a printing house and went to work with a will.

There was a young man at the printing house, whom Benjamin thought very good company. Admiring Franklin's skill in swimming this young man proposed that they should travel together through Europe, giving swimming lessons. Benjamin was quite pleased with the plan, and the first great American came very near becoming a swimming master. However, he decided to give up the idea and to return once more to Philadelphia.

For a while after he reached Philadelphia, Benjamin worked for his old employer, Keimer. But in a short time, through his good sense and thrifty habits, he was able to set up in business for himself. He was soon making a success of job printing, but he was not satisfied with this. His aims were higher.

At this time William Bradford printed the only newspaper in Pennsylvania, and that was a very poor one. In 1729, when Franklin was twenty-three years old, he decided that he would print a newspaper and make it the best in America.

He set vigorously to work. In a little while everyone wanted the *Pennsylvania Gazette*, for that was the name of the paper. It always had the best and latest news, although, as there were no railroads or telegraphs or telephones, this was not always very new. When there was not news enough to fill the paper, Franklin would write funny articles, which surprised and pleased the quiet old Quaker town. Sometimes he would ask funny questions in one paper and answer them himself in the next, pretending to be a different person each time.

Once Franklin published an article in his paper which some of the rich men of Philadelphia did not like. Hearing of their complaint Franklin invited the dissatisfied gentlemen to take supper with him. When they sat down at the table, they saw before them only two puddings made of corn meal, and a stone jug of water. Franklin politely helped his guests and then, filling his own plate, ate heartily. The guests tried to eat, but they were not used to such fare. At last Franklin rose and said, "My friends, anyone who can live on sawdust pudding and water, as I can, needs no man's patronage."

When Franklin was twenty-four he married Deborah Read, the girl who had laughed at him the first morning he came to Philadelphia. Mrs. Franklin was a true helpmate to her husband. He says, "She assisted me cheerfully in my business, folding and stitching pamphlets, tending shop, purchasing old linen rags for the paper makers," etc.

In those days everyone read the almanac very carefully. No matter how few books people had, they were sure to buy an almanac every year. In 1732, the very year that George Washington was born, Benjamin Franklin made up his mind to publish an almanac. It was to contain not only all the useful information usually found in almanacs, but also a great deal of wisdom, which should benefit the common people who bought scarcely any other books.

This almanac was called *Poor Richard's Almanack.* It was published for twenty-five years. In it, Franklin printed many funny pieces; but the things that are remembered best are the many wise sayings that he gathered together. Here are a few of them:

"Dost love thy life? Then do not squander time, for that is the stuff life is made of."

"The sleeping fox catches no poultry."

"Lost time is never found again."

"Laziness travels so slowly that poverty soon overtakes it."

"Early to bed and early to rise, makes a man healthy, wealthy, and wise."

Poor Richard, 1733.

A N

Almanack

For the Year of Chrift

1733,

Being the Firft after LEAP YEAR:

And makes fince the Creation	Years
By the Account of the Eaftern Greeks	7241
By the Latin Church, when ☉ ent. ♈	6932
By the Computation of W. W	5742
By the Roman Chronology	5682
By the Jewifh Rabbies	5494

Wherein is contained

The Lunations, Eclipfes, Judgment of the Weather, Spring Tides, Planets Motions & mutual Afpects, Sun and Moon's Rifing and Setting, Length of Days, Time of High Water, Fairs, Courts, and obfervable Days

Fitted to the Latitude of Forty Degrees, and a Meridian of Five Hours Weft from *London,* but may without fenfible Error, ferve all the adjacent Places, even from *Newfoundland* to *South-Carolina.*

By *RICHARD SAUNDERS*, Philom.

PHILADELPHIA:
Printed and fold by B. FRANKLIN, at the New Printing Office near the Market.

The Third Impreffion.

Facsimile of the Title Page of "Poor Richard's Almanack"

"One to-day is worth two to-morrows."

But you must find the rest of Poor Richard's sayings for yourself. How much the world thinks of them you may know by the fact that they have been translated into ten languages.

Franklin the Citizen

IN 1736 Franklin was elected to his first public office. He was made clerk of the General Assembly of Pennsylvania. The next year he was made deputy postmaster general. He now began to think considerably of public affairs, always planning something to help the common people.

The first thing that he did was to organize a better police force. Then he formed a fire company, the first in Philadelphia. This company had no engines or hose carts, as fire companies have to-day. Every member had to keep ready for use a certain number of leather water-buckets and some strong bags and baskets, in which to carry goods out of the burning house.

In Franklin's day all the houses were heated by great open fireplaces, near which you might sit and scorch your face while your back froze. Franklin invented an open stove which heated the entire room and at the same time saved fuel.

And, lover of learning that he was, he could not be satisfied to think that Pennsylvania had no college. In 1749 he succeeded in getting an academy founded.

This was the beginning of the present University of Pennsylvania. Philadelphia's public library, too, was started through Franklin's efforts.

Medal Portrait of Franklin Modeled
While He Was in France

Once a doctor came to him and asked him to help in establishing a hospital for poor sick people. The doctor said, "When I ask people to subscribe to this, they always say, 'Have you consulted Franklin, what does he think of it?'" The people of Pennsylvania had come to think that nothing could succeed without

Benjamin Franklin's good sense behind it. Franklin undertook the business and soon had established a Philadelphia hospital.

A great many more things were done for Pennsylvania, and especially for Philadelphia, by Franklin. He had the streets cleaned, paved, and lighted. He invented street lamps that did not smoke as the London lamps did.

Once when Franklin was in Boston, he met a man who showed him several electrical experiments. Franklin had known nothing of electricity before this time and was much interested in it.

A Dutchman living in the Dutch city of Leyden had discovered how to collect electricity in bottles, which he called Leyden jars. Franklin got one of these jars filled with electricity and soon had tried many experiments with it. His house was crowded with friends who came to see what he could do. He wrote a paper claiming that electricity and lightning were the same, and performed a famous experiment in proof of his belief.

He made a kite by fastening two cross sticks to a silk handkerchief. To the upright stick was fastened an iron point. The string of the kite was of common hemp, except the end which he held in his hand; this was of silk. Where hemp and silk were fastened together, a key was tied. When Franklin saw a thunderstorm coming he went out into the fields and raised the kite. A thundercloud passed over it; and, after a little, the loose fibers of the hemp string stood out stiffly. Franklin put his knuckles to the key and received a strong spark.

Then he tried to fill a Leyden jar with the electricity which came down the string, and he succeeded. Thus he had proved his theory.

Franklin's next invention was the lightning rod to protect houses from lightning by conducting electricity into the ground. Even King George III put lightning rods on his palace and on the royal powder magazines.

I must tell you about one of Franklin's experiments, which came near being disastrous. One night he was about to kill a turkey by the shock from two large Leyden jars, when he thoughtlessly took hold of the apparatus and received the whole shock through his body. For a little while he lost his senses entirely. His words upon coming to himself were, "Well, I meant to kill a turkey, and instead I nearly killed a goose."

In 1753 Franklin was made postmaster general of the colonies, and made many improvements in the postal service.

The people of the colonies now began to see that the French were pushing their way to the headwaters of the Ohio and down Lake Champlain from the north, and that they were determined to profit by the discoveries which Champlain and La Salle had made many years before. Something must be done to stop the French, so the English colonies sent men to Albany to meet the chiefs of the Iroquois (the old enemies of the French) and to find means of holding the country. Pennsylvania sent Franklin as her representative to the convention. On the way to Albany, Franklin made a plan for the union of the colonies under one government.

When the convention met, several plans were talked over, and it was decided that Franklin's was the best. But when the scheme was laid before the different colonies they did not like it because, they said, "it did not give the colonists enough power." And when it was laid before the people of England, they said it gave the colonists too much power. So the plan, wise as it was, was not adopted.

The Handwriting of Franklin

In 1757 the descendants of William Penn still governed Pennsylvania. They were not at all like William Penn, for they treated the people very badly. By this time war with the French was on in earnest. The taxes were very high. The Penns were rich and had a great deal of valuable land in Pennsylvania, but they would pay no taxes and compelled the poor people to bear the heavy expenses of the war. So the people of Pennsylvania sent Benjamin Franklin to England to ask the King to take the government of Pennsylvania away from the Penns and to govern it himself.

When Franklin arrived in England he found that everyone knew about him there because of his discoveries in electricity and his clever writings. The English people were more willing to listen to him than to any other American, and the King finally took the government into his own hands, as Franklin asked him to do.

However when several years later the war between the colonies and the French came to an end, the Penns again refused to pay their share of the heavy taxes. So once more Franklin was sent to England to complain.

This time he stayed more than ten years. When he came back his faithful wife was dead, his daughter was married, and he himself was an old man. The battle of Lexington had been fought, and the farmers at Concord had "fired the shot heard round the world." The American Revolution had begun.

As soon as Franklin got back to America he was sent as a delegate to the Second Continental Congress; and he was one of the five men chosen to prepare the Declaration of Independence, which was signed July 4, 1776, making the United States of America an independent nation.

As the members of the Congress were signing the Declaration, John Hancock, who wrote his name so large, "that the King of England could read it without spectacles," said, "We must all hang together."

"Yes," said Franklin, "we must hang together or we shall hang separately."

Independence Hall, Philadelphia, in 1776

You must remember that while England was a very rich and powerful nation the United States was very poor indeed. So her Congress decided to send to France to ask for aid in her fight for liberty. In all America there was just one man who could persuade the French people to help the United States, and Congress knew it. They sent Benjamin Franklin, seventy years old, and suffering with rheumatism and gout. "I am old and good for nothing," he said; "as the storekeepers say of their remnants of cloth, I am but a fag end; you may have me for what you please."

When Franklin got to Paris he found the whole city ready to receive him. Everyone had heard of the great

Dr. Franklin.

But while fame was plenty, money was scarce. Franklin had to be very careful and very wise indeed to get the help which the United States needed. Finally, in 1778, the French signed a treaty promising ships, men, and money. You may be sure the news of that treaty was most welcome to George Washington. While Washington was fighting at home at the head of the American army, the brave old doctor, in far away France, had secured food and ammunition for the starving soldiers, and shoes for their bleeding feet.

In 1781 the glad news reached Paris that the English general, Cornwallis, had surrendered to General Washington at Yorktown. The war was over. In 1783 men from America and England met in Paris to make the treaty of peace. Through all this time Benjamin Franklin's wise counsel was serving his country well.

It was not until 1785 that Franklin came home for the last time. He was so feeble that he could not ride in a carriage and had to be taken from Paris to the sea-coast, a distance of one hundred and fifty miles, in the "Queen's litter," a kind of covered couch carried between two mules. When the ship reached Philadelphia all the bells of the city were rung, and cannon were fired in honor of his safe arrival.

When he had been home but a few weeks Franklin was elected president of Pennsylvania. Old and weak as he was, the people would not let him off. "They have eaten my flesh," he said jokingly, "and now they are picking my bones."

In 1787 Franklin performed his last duty to his country. The wise men of the United States met in Philadelphia to make the Constitution, and Franklin was chosen one of the delegates.

In 1790 the first great American passed away. His work lives after him in the nation that he did so much to build.

XXIV

MONTCALM AND WOLFE

French and Indian Wars

By the middle of the eighteenth century the colonies of England and France were firmly planted in North America. Along the courses of two great rivers—the St. Lawrence and the Mississippi—the French had crept in and made settlements, strengthening themselves by mighty forts along the St. Lawrence, and by a straggling chain of weaker ones along the Mississippi. And what a great country the claim of these two rivers gave the French; all the wilderness region watered by the Mississippi and its branches; all the valley of the St. Lawrence, the Great Lakes, and Lake Champlain.

To offset this mighty empire, England had a narrow strip of Atlantic seacoast, settled by thirteen colonies. Doesn't it seem that England's claim was small beside that of France? But remember that although it was only the coast region that was settled, England claimed that her colonies extended straight across North America to the Pacific Ocean.

If you will look at your map, you will see that a

great deal of the land claimed by France and England was the very same land. The French claimed the entire Mississippi valley; the English claimed the greater part of it. The French claimed all the region of the Great Lakes, including a good part of the present State of New York, while the English claimed a great deal of the lake region for themselves, including all of New York.

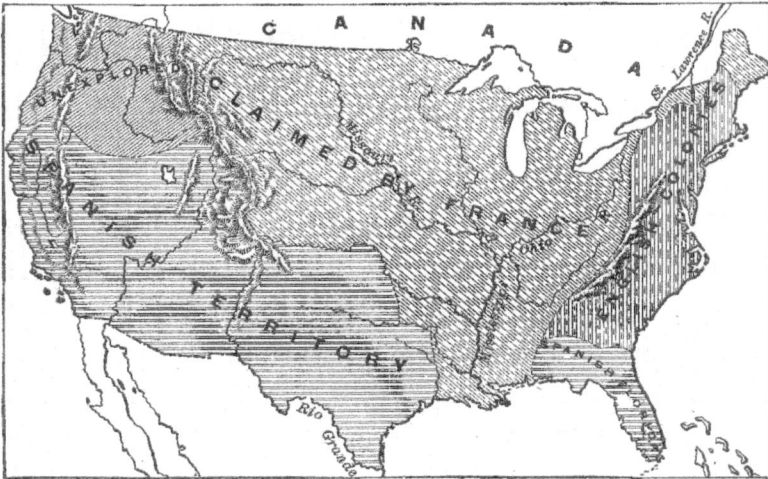

The Present Territory of the United States as Claimed by the French, English, and Spanish in 1749

As France and England were usually fighting with each other at home, one could hardly expect that their colonies could live at peace in America, especially when both claimed the same territory. War had to come, and war came.

There were four wars between the French and the English in America, lasting off and on from 1689 to 1763. The last one was the most important; it settled matters for all time.

There were about fourteen times as many English in America as there were French. But the French balanced this disadvantage by the help of many tribes of bloodthirsty Indians. The English, on the other hand, had only the Iroquois to help them.

It was in the year 1749 that the very beginnings of the last war between the French and the English in America were made. The French Governor of Canada saw that the daring English settlers were pushing their way westward into the Ohio valley. If once a colony of English should get firmly planted in the valley of the Ohio, it would be an easy thing for them to get between the French of Canada and the French of Louisiana. Thus the English could creep north and south and attack the French from the very heart of the country they called their own.

This invading of the French claims along the Ohio continued and was greatly troubling the French when the Marquis Duquesne was sent as the new governor of Canada.

"We will go straight down to the Ohio country," said Governor Duquesne, "and build strong forts."

So a French expedition set out. First, they stopped on the shore of Lake Erie, where the city of Erie now stands, and built a fort of chestnut logs. Then they made a road through the woods to French Creek, where they built another fort, which they called Fort Le Bœuf.

Here they were much surprised to see a tall young man on horseback coming out of the woods with a dozen white men and Indians. The young man's name was George Washington, and he brought a letter from Governor Dinwiddie of Virginia. "Will you please tell me," said the letter, "what right you have on land which belongs to the King of England? I must ask you to leave at once."

The French treated young Major Washington very well during his three days' stay at the fort. But they refused to leave.

When Washington returned to Governor Dinwiddie he told him that he had found a splendid place for a fort. This was at the forks of the Ohio, where Pittsburg now stands.

Governor Dinwiddie had a hard time to get the English colonies interested in the encroachments of the French. "The French are not troubling us," they said. "Let them have the Ohio country. We have our own affairs to look after." The colonies had not yet learned to hang together.

While he was trying to stir up the half-hearted colonies to see their danger, Governor Dinwiddie sent young Washington to occupy the Ohio country. A group of backwoodsmen were to go ahead and build the fort at the forks of the Ohio.

Working on their fort, these men saw a great swarm of boats floating down the Monongahela. The boats were full of Frenchmen. "We will save you the trouble of building your fort," said the Frenchmen. The backwoodsmen fled over the mountains to meet Washington, while the French tore down their fort and

Washington in His Colonel's Uniform

Painted in 1772. The earliest portrait known of Washington.

built a bigger and better one. This they named Fort Duquesne, after the Governor of Canada.

When Washington heard that the French were building Fort Duquesne, he knew that a battle must

*The English Route to
Fort Duquesne*

soon be expected. So he selected a level piece of land covered with grass and bushes, with a ravine on one side. He called the place "Great Meadows" and set his men to prepare it for a battlefield. For several days Indians and back-woodsmen came in, reporting that Frenchmen were skulking about. Finally Washington found a small body of the enemy hiding in a rocky hollow. Washington attacked these, and all but one of them were killed or taken prisoners. This was the beginning of the last and greatest war between the French and the English.

Realizing that as soon as the news reached Fort Duquesne a large body of French would be sent against him, Washington built a rude fort, which he named Fort Necessity, and there waited for the enemy.

The French had several times as many men as Washington had. And besides, Washington's men were half starved, and their powder was wet. They fought bravely, but finally Washington saw that it would be useless to keep on. He surrendered, sick at heart. The French permitted him and his men to leave the fort with the honors of war, taking all their property with them. So many of the men were sick or wounded that every man who was able had to carry a comrade on his back.

The French marched triumphantly back to Fort Duquesne, burning all the buildings they found on their way. Not an English flag was left to wave west of the Alleghanies.

Then the English colonies began to wake up, and now it was that they sent men to Albany to talk things over and to make a treaty with the Iroquois. Here Hendrick, the chief of the Iroquois, made a stirring speech to the colonists: "Look about your country and see," he said. "You have no fortifications, no, not even in this city. It is but a step from here to Canada, and the French may come and turn you out of doors. Look at the French; they are men; they are fortifying everywhere. But you are all like women."

The Indians spoke only too truly. A line of strong French forts extended from the mouth of the St. Lawrence to the Ohio; and there were two, Ticonderoga and Crown Point, near the southern extremity of Lake Champlain, very close to Albany itself.

In the meantime England herself saw that something must be done. It was decided that all of the strongest forts of the French must be attacked. This was the plan: General Braddock was to take soldiers from England and capture Fort Duquesne; Governor Shirley of Massachusetts was to take a body of colonists and attack Fort Niagara; Colonel William Johnson, who lived on the Mohawk, and had great influence with the Indians, was to attack Crown Point; and another army of colonists was to attack Acadia, or Nova Scotia, as it is now called.

In February, 1755, General Braddock with his well-drilled redcoats, reached Virginia. Horses and wagons were very scarce in Virginia, and it seemed for some time as if it would be impossible to find any way to carry the supplies that would be needed by the large army on the march.

But Benjamin Franklin, who always knew how to do the right thing at the right time, went to the farmers of Pennsylvania and persuaded them to furnish wagons and horses, and the army finally started for Fort Duquesne.

When Braddock reached Wills Creek he found that the army of Virginia soldiers had been doing good work. A solid log fort stood here, armed with ten small cannon. When Braddock drew up his army in the clearing in front of the fort, it was an impressive sight. There were fourteen hundred English soldiers in their bright red uniforms, and about five hundred awkward Virginians, among whom was that bravest Virginian of all, George Washington.

Braddock was a brave man, but he did not like to listen to other people's advice. When Washington told him of the Indian ways of fighting, he laughed and said that trained British soldiers could not learn warfare from ignorant savages. When some of the Indians came and offered to join Braddock's army he treated them coldly. "He looked upon us as dogs," said one of their chiefs, "and would never hear anything that we said to him."

Once more the army was started on the march. Three hundred axmen went ahead to clear the way. Suddenly the English army came upon the French near Fort Duquesne. The battle was on in an instant, and when it was ended Braddock had been terribly defeated. His red-coated soldiers had proved an easy mark for the French and Indians. When the firing had commenced, Braddock had drawn up his men in fine battle array, as he had been accustomed to do upon the battlefields of Europe. But from behind every tree and bush the fire of an invisible enemy fell upon his helpless soldiers. They huddled together like sheep, not knowing which way to fire. "We would fight," they cried, "if we could see anyone to fight with."

Braddock showed himself a brave general, if not a wise one. Four horses were shot under him, and he fell from the fifth with a deadly wound through his lungs. "Leave me where I am," he cried; but the officers bore him away to safety. He died several days later. "We shall know better the next time," were his last words.

There was another courageous fighter on that battlefield, and that was young George Washington. He was everywhere, cheering the men, making the best of a bad matter. Two horses were killed under him, and four bullets passed through his coat, but he was unharmed.

Montcalm and Wolfe—The Close of the War

BRADDOCK'S defeat at Fort Duquesne was a crushing blow to England and her colonies. The attack upon Niagara was scarcely more successful, and that upon Crown Point amounted to little.

Although the English did not seem to be making much headway, the French decided that the best of soldiers should be sent to America. The French king looked about for a good general to command the French forces in America, and he chose Louis de Montcalm, one of the best soldiers and truest gentlemen in all France.

When Montcalm was a boy at school he wrote to his father and told him what his ambitions were. "First," he said, "I want to be an honorable man, of good morals, brave, and a Christian." This ambition Louis de Montcalm realized, unlike most of the Frenchmen of his day. He was a dutiful and obedient son, and a loving husband and father.

Besides the French soldiers who came with Montcalm, all the men of Canada, between the ages of fifteen and sixty, were enrolled in the militia, to be ready to fight whenever they were wanted, and to these were added many Indians.

The only important victory of 1756 was won by Montcalm. This was the capture of the English fort at Oswego. Oswego was one of the strongest and most important of the English forts, as it was located on Lake

Ontario; and its loss was a great blow to the English.

The next year Montcalm struck another important blow. News came that the best of the English troops had gone to attack Louisburg. Louisburg was the strongest of the French forts, and, besides Quebec, the most important, for it stood at the entrance of the St. Lawrence. This expedition left the two English forts, Fort William Henry, on Lake George, and Fort Edward, on the Hudson, without strong protection.

This was just what Montcalm wanted. He sent messengers to the north and west to gather the Indians into Montreal. More than a thousand came and encamped around the city. Many of them had never before seen a French settlement. All were eager to see Montcalm, for they had heard of his capture of Oswego. One of the chiefs said to him, "We wanted to see the famous man who tramples the English under his feet. We thought we would find him so tall that his head would be lost in the clouds. But you are a little man, my father. It is when we look into your eyes that we see the greatness of the pine tree and the fire of the eagle."

With a body of eight thousand men Montcalm marched to Ticonderoga. Among his troops were some of the finest gentlemen of Europe, as well as some of the cruelest savages of America. All were bound upon the same errand. "Let us trample the English under our feet," was the war song which the Indians made the Frenchmen sing with them before they would agree to start upon the expedition.

From Ticonderoga Montcalm proceeded south and placed his army between Fort William Henry and Fort Edward, in order to prevent the soldiers of Fort Edward from coming to help defend Fort William Henry.

The Indians gave the French much trouble. They always complained that not enough notice was taken of them, and that, instead of being consulted about the siege, they were expected to obey orders, like slaves. "We know more about fighting in the woods than you," they said. Finally, the siege began. The Indians forgot their discontent in the sound of cannon roaring through the forest. Sometimes the Indians would be allowed to point the cannon, much to their delight.

After a siege of three days, the men defending Fort William Henry saw that there was no hope of receiving aid from any direction. A white flag was raised, a drum was beaten, and one of the English officers left the fort and approached Montcalm's tent. Montcalm agreed that the English should march out with the honors of war, and that they should be taken to Fort Edward the next day under the protection of French soldiers.

Montcalm called a council of the Indian chiefs and made them promise not to allow the English to be hurt. The chiefs promised, but the promise was kept in a savage fashion. The next morning, before the

French were stirring, they fell upon the English, and commenced a terrible massacre. Montcalm rushed out at the first news of disturbance and threw himself among the Indians, crying, "Kill me, but spare the English who are under my protection." But even their general's bravery was useless among these savages. Montcalm found that it was easier to lead Indians to battle than to lead them away from it. He was glad indeed when his army once more turned toward Montreal.

In the meantime, the English expedition against Louisburg had failed. At the end of the year 1757 the fortunes of the English looked very dark indeed.

That year a new prime minister was put at the head of affairs in England. This was William Pitt, a very wise man, who understood America better than most English people did. "Something has to be done," said he.

In 1758 he planned three campaigns. "First," he said, "we must take Louisburg, as the first step toward taking Quebec. Then we must capture Ticonderoga, which is right in the heart of the northern colonies. Next we must take Fort Duquesne, the key to the great West."

General Amherst was sent to attack Louisburg, and with him came a young brigadier, named James Wolfe. James Wolfe was the son of an officer in the English army. Although very delicate in health, he had longed from earliest childhood to be a soldier. At fifteen he had entered the army, and at sixteen had served as adjutant of his regiment in Flanders. He passed through several military campaigns in Scotland, and at twenty-three was made a lieutenant colonel. All this time he had kept up a constant battle with ill health. He was a great student, and spent all his spare time in study.

Like Montcalm, Wolfe loved his mother very dearly and confided to her all his hopes and ambitions. "The greatest happiness that I wish for is to see you happy," he wrote in one of his letters to her. And again, "If you stay much at home I will come and shut myself up with you for three weeks or a month, and you shall laugh at my short red hair as much as you please." Once he said to her, "All I wish for myself is that I may at all times be ready to die, and may die properly when the hour comes." How that wish came true you may judge for yourself.

Louisburg was indeed the strongest fort in America, but this time the men who had come to attack it were very determined. They meant to win. Of these the bravest and most eager for danger was young Brigadier Wolfe, and there were none who won greater honors there. After a long and stubborn siege, the fort was taken by the English, with almost six thousand French prisoners.

The English capture of Louisburg meant a great loss to the French. It gave the English the key to the St. Lawrence. They could now sail straight up to Quebec.

This, Wolfe wanted to do at once. He had no patience with the slow movements of the older English generals.

The English attack upon Ticonderoga did not succeed. The English leader, Lord Howe, was killed before the siege fairly began. Montcalm defended the fort and fought fearlessly; wherever danger was greatest he was always to be seen, directing everything, and encouraging his men. The French won the day.

William Pitt Advises Young James Wolfe
Before He Sails for Canada

This, however, was the last triumph which the French were to have. Before the end of 1758, Fort Duquesne and Fort Frontenac had both fallen into the hands of the English.

There remained yet the one great stronghold of the French, the rock-walled city of Quebec. If Quebec were to be taken, the St. Lawrence would belong to the

English. In 1759 Pitt appointed for this purpose the very man who most longed to attack Quebec, young James Wolfe, now only thirty-two years old.

By May, Wolfe had his fleet collected in the harbor of Louisburg. In June they sailed out, the troops cheering and crying, "British colors on every French fort, post, and garrison in America!"

In Quebec, Montcalm was making great preparations to receive his unwelcome guests. Sixteen thousand men, including French soldiers, Canadians, and Indians, poured into the city. All along the borders of the St. Lawrence, Montcalm had men throwing up defenses. Every gate of the city, except the river gate, was closed and barricaded. More than one hundred cannon were mounted on the walls, while gunboats and fire ships lay along the river. Fortified upon that high rock, Quebec seemed like a great eagle's nest far beyond the reach of men.

Wolfe entered the St. Lawrence and landed, leaving his fleet anchored in the river. Montcalm saw this, and had the fire ships, filled with tar, pitch, old iron, and gunpowder, lighted and set afloat down the river. For a time the English on the ships were frightened. But the fire ships did the English no harm; some drifted ashore before they reached the English fleet, and the rest were pushed away by the grappling hooks of the bold English sailors.

Wolfe had landed, but could find no way to get at the enemy. From lofty Quebec, Montcalm could watch the movements of the British; and he decided that it was safer to watch them than offer battle. Wolfe finally took up his position on a height opposite Quebec. Here he waited and watched for an opportunity to attack Montcalm. Besides, he hoped for reënforcements.

The Citadel of Quebec and the Plains of Abraham

But the reënforcements did not come, and, on the other hand, there seemed to be no way to provoke Montcalm to battle. Wolfe's old sickness came upon him, and his officers feared that he would never live to see more fighting. But he got better again, and even tried to be cheerful.

One day in September Wolfe set out with his spy-glass and sailed up and down the river, studying the steep side of the rock of Quebec. He spied a narrow and rugged ravine, leading up the side of the rock. At once he formed a daring plan.

That night the boats of the English floated silently down the river. Landing, Wolfe, at the head of the

English troops, scrambled up the narrow ravine which he had seen during the day. Drawing themselves up by the roots and branches of trees, they reached the top. In the gray of the morning the young commander lined up his red-coated soldiers on the Plains of Abraham, with the city directly in front of him.

"They come! They come!" cried a swift runner to Montcalm. "Who come?" asked Montcalm, in surprise.

"The English!" was the excited reply, and "The English!" was echoed in terror throughout the city.

One of the Gates of the Old Citadel of Quebec

It seemed impossible, but it was true. The French general drew up his troops to meet the English, in front of the walls of Quebec. "I remember well how he looked," said one of the Canadians many years after. "He rode a black horse along the front of our lines, brandishing his sword, as if to excite us to do our duty."

Wolfe too was everywhere, encouraging the men, kind and thoughtful to the wounded, praising the brave.

270

As he was leading a charge at the head of his grenadiers, a shot shattered his wrist. He wrapped his handkerchief about it and went on. Another shot struck him, but he still kept on. A third lodged in his breast. He staggered and, as he fell, was caught in the arms of his soldiers. They carried him to the rear.

"Will you have a surgeon?" they asked.

"There's no need," he said. "It's all over with me." A moment later one of the men cried, "They run! See how they run!"

Wolfe raised himself for the last time. "Who run?" he asked.

"The enemy, sir; they give way everywhere."

"Now, God be praised, I die in peace," said the dying man.

A few moments later Montcalm, on his gallant black horse, was shot through the body. A soldier caught him on each side and led his horse through the city gates.

"It is nothing, nothing," said Montcalm. "Don't be troubled for me, my good friends."

"How long have I to live?" he asked the surgeon a little later.

"Twelve hours," was the answer. "So much the better," he said. "I am happy that I shall not live to see the surrender of Quebec."

The capture of Quebec by the English was the last blow to French power in America. One nation was wild with joy, and one bitter with grief. In far-away England

and France two homes mourned apart. Two mothers were weeping for their cherished sons, whose lives had been given for their countries.

The final settlement of the war between France and England came with the Treaty of Paris, made in 1763. By its terms France ceded to England all her American possessions east of the Mississippi River, with the exception of two small islands near the Newfoundland coast. Thus ended French rule on the American continent.

XXV

SIR WILLIAM JOHNSON

RIGHT across the present state of New York lay the land of the mighty Iroquois Indians. Five tribes formed this race, the Mohawks, the Oneidas, the Onondagas, the Cayugas and the Senecas. In the whole of America no Indians were more ferocious or more powerful than the Iroquois. Living at peace with one another the Five Nations, with their combined strength, made a terrible foe for the enemy. (Later the Iroquois adopted a sixth tribe into their confederacy. This sixth tribe were the Tuscaroras.)

Through the beautiful Mohawk Valley and on west to Niagara they built their Long Houses, roved at will and lived their free wild life. The land was theirs.

Then came the time when the French settled Quebec, and down from the north came Champlain and his Algonquin war party. All unsuspecting and sure of success the Iroquois rushed into battle. When, behold, a white man—unheard of wonder—appeared in the lead of the old familiar enemy, and with his death-dealing gun killed in one instant two great Iroquois chiefs! For the first time panic filled the breasts of their followers and, in terror, they fled before the white man from the north.

The Dutch, settling at first to the south of the Iroquois' land, dealt more peaceably with the Five Nations. From their trading posts on the Hudson they carried on a lively fur trade with the red men; and with the Mohawks, formed a treaty of peace. But, for all the friendly relations, the fact remained that gradually, gradually the white men were shutting in the Iroquois on the south and east as well as on the north and west.

And, still, the newcomers were not content. After the Dutch had surrendered to the English, England's king began selling to his subjects great tracts of land right in the Mohawk valley itself. The Indians watched this spreading out with a jealous eye. Surely, here was cause for trouble between the English settlers and the savages.

One of these estates, lying on the south side of the Mohawk river, was bought by a certain Sir Peter Warren, an admiral in the English navy. And Sir Peter sent his nephew, William Johnson, to live on this American property and look after its owner's interests. A more fortunate choice could not have been made.

William Johnson was an Irish lad born in that country in 1715. "William is a Spritely Boy, well grown, of good parts, Keen wit but Most Onruly and Streperous!" says Sir Peter's diary of William when he was eleven. The good qualities must have over-balanced the bad ones as the boy grew up, for Sir Peter would hardly have made an "onruly and streperous" person his American agent.

It was December, 1737, when William Johnson reached New York. There he spent the winter making plans and laying in supplies to be used in his new life. With the spring he set out for his uncle's estate. Here he built a storehouse and a dwelling and here he lived for five years clearing the land, making roads, selling farms and doing all he could to better the property and enrich his uncle.

Soon he began to buy for himself land north of the Mohawk and, at the end of his first five years, he moved into a great stone house built on his own property at Akin. This new home, which is still standing, Johnson called "Mount Johnson."

All this was very well for Sir Peter and for William Johnson, but it is not what makes him important in our history. You see from the very first William Johnson took a lively interest in the Indians. He learned their language, invited them time and again to his home, traded with them for furs, paid them for the land he bought, hunted with them, fished with them and, above all, treated them always fairly and squarely. Such dealings were so unlike what they were used to from other traders that it won for Johnson the rare love of the red men. And one day, dressed in the height of Indian fashion, and entering into the very spirit of the occasion, he was formally adopted into the Mohawk tribe and made an Indian Chief! Naturally, this only increased his already great influence over the Indians.

How William Johnson contrived to humor his wily

friends and yet keep the upper hand of them, you can see. Once King Hendrick, great Iroquois Chief that he was, while visiting Johnson saw a richly gold-embroidered coat. How he wanted that coat! He could not get it out of his mind. So, in a few days, back he came and said to Johnson, "Brother, I dream. I dream you gave me your coat of gold." Johnson smiled at the old chief and said, "Well, I suppose you must have it then," and without any hesitation gave King Hendrick the coveted coat. Then, in his turn, Johnson tried the same scheme, and next time he saw the king said, "I too dream." "And what was your dream?" asked the chief. "I dreamed you gave me all the land between the East and West Canada Creek." It was pretty hard for even an Indian to show no feeling at such a demand, but as calmly as possible King Hendrick said, "Well, I suppose you must have it, but, brother, we will quit dreaming." This land has been called "Sir William Johnson's Dreamland Tract." He later made the Indians a present of enough money to pay them for the land.

Seeing how he managed the Indians, the colonial governor, in 1746, appointed Johnson Superintendent of Indian Affairs for the Colony of New York, and the appointment was confirmed by the king himself. Later Johnson was made General Superintendent of Indian Affairs for the country.

This position was one of great and growing importance. As long as the Iroquois could be kept friendly to the English, see what a protesting wall they made during the wars with the French and their allied Canadian tribes. Were it not for just this wall, the enemy could easily ravage most of New York at will. And soon after Johnson became Superintendent of Indian Affairs, the disputes which led to the last French and Indian war began.

Imagine the alarm when rumors reached Johnson that French messengers were visiting the tribes in the west of the colony, stirring up discontent and seeking to turn them against the English. Although it was December, cold and snowy; although part of the 160-mile journey was over no better road than an Indian trail, Johnson set out on horseback at once. From village to village he rode till he came to the "Keepers of the Western Door," as the Senecas were called. Here, as everywhere, he was heartily welcomed by his Indian friends and given the best their homes could boast. Whatever damage the French messengers had done was more than offset now, and once more Johnson felt sure of the loyalty of the Iroquois.

When the Albany Convention met in 1754 to discuss plans for colonial protection, the Iroquois further proved their loyalty by sending representatives and pledging their help, providing William Johnson should be their leader. And, true to their word, when Major General Johnson led an attack on Crown Point, several hundred Indians formed part of his force.

Starting north from Fort Edward, Johnson met the French at the head of Lake George. A desperate battle was fought, Johnson and the French Commander both being wounded and the brave old Indian king, Hendrick, killed. Although the French were at last beaten and driven back, Crown Point was still in the enemy's hands. The main effect of Johnson's victory was to encourage the English, who were still sorely depressed over Braddock's defeat of a few weeks before.

Another victory fell to Johnson's lot when in 1759 Fort Niagara surrendered to the army under his command. As a reward for his services in the French and Indian war England knighted him.

After the war was over Sir William built a beautiful new home called "Johnson Hall" where stands the Johnstown of to-day. By this time, he was the owner of many thousand of acres north of the Mohawk. Hardly had he moved into his new home when more trouble arose.

It was discovered that Pontiac, chief of a Michigan tribe friendly to the French, had been forming a league of many tribes and inciting them to drive the English from their land. In 1763 fort after fort was attacked in the west. Most of these attacks came with no warning and, whenever the Indians were victorious, they joyfully murdered the garrison.

Detroit might have met the same fate but for the loyalty of a beautiful Indian girl. Slipping inside the fortifications on a trumped up errand, she warned the Commander that Pontiac was coming next day with sixty chiefs to ask that a council be held. Each chief would be wrapped in his blanket and hidden in its folds he would carry a gun. Pontiac would make a friendly speech and then offer a wampum belt. When he held out this supposed token of peace, the chiefs were to throw off their blankets, spring upon the officers and scalp and kill until not an Englishman was left alive.

Sure enough, next morning Pontiac and his blanketed chiefs appeared, their faces painted, their eyes gleaming. But, what was their surprise to see the English officers lined up inside the fortifications fully armed. And even in the council house every officer had a sword at his side and a pistol in his belt. Pontiac needed no interpreter to tell him that his plot was known. The wampum belt was not presented and, after a little, the meeting broke up and the savage chiefs stalked away as they had come. This was in May, and after their all-summer siege, Detroit was still in English possession.

During all this widespread revolt Sir William Johnson was able to keep most of the Iroquois in control. A few of the Senecas did go out on the war path, but the other tribes remained loyal to their English friends.

The spring of 1764 brought more ravaging of the English borders by the western Indians. However, in June, Sir William succeeded by coaxing or threats in gathering together a great Indian council at Niagara. There, dealing with one tribe after another, he induced them to give up fighting the English and to sign treaties of peace. But, though the backbone of Pontiac's rebellion was now broken, it was not until two years later that that great chief himself finally met Sir William at Oswego, smoked the peace pipe and buried the tomahawk.

The last years of Sir William Johnson's life were for the most part spent at Johnson Hall. Even when he was dying there in the summer of 1774, his thoughts seemed to be with his Indian friends. And it was with almost his last breath that turning his eyes to Joseph Brant, the Iroquois chief, he said, "Joseph, control your people—control your people! I am going away."

CHRONOLOGY

circa 1000. The Northmen explore the mainland of North America.

1271-1295. Marco Polo visits China.

1492. Columbus discovers the West Indies (San Salvador).

1497. The Cabots discover the North American continent.

1498. Columbus on his third voyage discovers South America.

1507. The New World named after Americus Vespucius.

1513. Ponce de Leon claims Florida for Spain. Balboa discovers the Pacific Ocean.

1519-1521. Cortez conquers Mexico.

1519-1522. Magellan's ships sail around the world.

1524. Verrazano explores the Atlantic coast from North Carolina to Newfoundland.

1525-1541. Pizarro explores, conquers, and rules Peru.

1535. Cartier discovers the St. Lawrence River.

1541. De Soto discovers the Mississippi.

1562-1565. French Huguenots under Ribaut, and Laudonnière attempt settlements on the South Atlantic coast.

1565.   Spaniards under Menendez make the settlement of St. Augustine.

1577-1580.   Sir Francis Drake sails around the world.

1579.   Drake explores the coast of California.

1578-1583.   Sir Humphrey Gilbert attempts to plant a colony in North America and explores the coast from Newfoundland to the Kennebec River.

1584-1587.   Sir Walter Raleigh sends an exploring expedition to the eastern coast of America and attempts a settlement on Roanoke Island.

1604.   Acadia settled by the French.

1607.   Expedition sent out by the London Company makes the settlement of Jamestown.

1608.   Champlain founds Quebec.

1609.   Henry Hudson explores the Hudson River.

1610.   Henry Hudson reaches Hudson Bay.

1613.   First settlements made by the Dutch, on Manhattan Island.

1619.   Slavery introduced into Virginia.

1620.   The Pilgrims land at Plymouth.

1628.   First settlement of Puritans at Salem, Massachusetts.

1630.   Governor Winthrop and Puritans come to New England and found Boston.

1634.   English Roman Catholics under Lord Baltimore found Maryland and make the first settlement at St. Mary's.

1636. Roger Williams founds Providence.

1637. Pequot War.

1638. Delaware settled by the Swedes.

1664. The Dutch surrender New Netherland to the English.

1673. Joliet and Marquette journey down the Mississippi.

1675. King Philip's War.

1676. Bacon's Rebellion and the burning of Jamestown.

1681. English Quakers under William Penn colonize Pennsylvania.

1682. The Quakers under Penn found Philadelphia.

1682. La Salle explores the Mississippi to the Gulf of Mexico and claims Louisiana for France.

1733. English (mostly debtors) under Oglethorpe found Georgia and make the first settlement at Savannah.

1749-1763. Last of the French and Indian Wars.

1754. Colonial Congress at Albany; Franklin's plan of union.

1755. Braddock's defeat at Fort Duquesne.

1757. French capture Forts William Henry and Ticonderoga.

1758. English capture Forts Duquesne and Frontenac.

1759. Siege of Quebec.

1763. Treaty of Paris.

www.ingramcontent.com/pod-product-compliance
Lightning Source LLC
Chambersburg PA
CBHW032037080426
42733CB00006B/111